JN082346

ウェンデリン・ファン・オルデンボルフ

柔らかな舞台

目次

ウェンデリン・ファン・オルデンボルフの流動的なトポス ── 崔 敬華 ── 7

不透明なフェミニスト／クィア・ポリフォニー ── 菅野優香 ── 23

我々が集う時 ── ビンナ・チョイ ── 43

考察のイメージ ── パブロ・デ・オカンポ ── 67

ウェンデリン・ファン・オルデンボルフ：インタビュー ── アンドリュー・マークル ── 91

作品リスト・解説 ── 115

ウェンデリン・ファン・オルデンボルフの流動的なトポス

崔 敬華

東京都現代美術館学芸員

ウェンデリン・ファン・オルデンボルフはこれまで二十年以上にわたり、支配的な言説や権力構造に対峙するパフォーマティビティ（行為遂行性）を表出する方法としての映像制作をベースに、多角的な実践に取り組んできた。制作では、ある歴史的問題や社会的課題に関連するロケーション、資料や他の素材、キャストやクルーとして参加する人々を選び、撮影現場で繰り広げられる会話やコミュニケーションを記録する。そこで発露する人々の主観性や関係性を複雑に絡み合うアッサンブラージュに編成し、取り上げられる問題に対する複数の視座や感性を提示する。

映像制作を通じて人々の主観性や差異の現れの場を生成しようとするファン・オルデンボルフの試みは、二十年以上自国を離れて暮らしながら、特にブラジルとの個人的な繋がりを形成したのちに、オランダへと戻り、映画制作の形式を取り入れて組織した《あるブラジル人らしさ》（二〇〇四―二〇〇八年）から始まった。差異を豊かさと捉え、国家主義的かつ統一的なアイデンティティを否定したブラジルのモダニズム運動をモチーフとしたこの領域横断的なプロジェクトは、調和を目的化することなく、他者との水平的な関係を構築し交渉する場を形成することを試み、プロジェクトの参加者と鑑賞者が互いの役割と立場を行き来しながら、ヒップホップのジャム・セッション、トークといった共同作業を記録し、発表する複数のイベントを行った。本展で展示した2チャンネル・インスタレーション《マウリッツ・スクリプト》（二〇〇六年）はこのプロジェクトのひとつの段階で制作され、彼女のその後の映像制作の展望を切り拓いたとも言える。

この作品では、異なるバックグラウンドを持つ人々がキャストやクルーとして、ハーグのマウリッツハ

崔 敬華

イス美術館で行った公開撮影に参加し、十七世紀にオランダ領ブラジルを統治したヨハン・マウリッツ・ファン・ナッサウに関する資料を読み、その歴史編纂と、現代の社会システムに息づく植民地時代の権力の遺構について検証する。二面スクリーンの片方は、参加者がこの歴史に関わる人物の言葉を朗読する様子を、もう一方は、オランダ社会での自らの経験や知識や心的状況を共有し議論する様子を映し出す。カメラは、彼ら彼女らのそれとない振る舞いや、語り手の話を聞きながらつくる表情などにしばしばフォーカスを当てる。また、議論の合間やフレームの内と外にいる人々によって起こる偶発的な出来事や些細な瞬間——美術館の来館者が撮影に出くわす場面や、ファン・オルデンボルフが参加者の会話に介入する姿、マイクブーム、カメラ、化粧道具を持ったクルーたちが動き回る様子など——を捉え、制御と自発性の興味深い相互作用を織り成す。

ファン・オルデンボルフのシネマトグラフィーと編集は、他の作品でも同様に、映画的な整合性を構築することに重きを置いていない。むしろ、自己を再審するようにアーティスト自らを含めた俯瞰的なショットや、突飛な断絶や、極端に接近したショットなどを挿入しながら、筋書きを持った物語や表象から逸脱し続ける。撮影という場を構築する自らの営為性を露わにしながら、キャストやクルーがどのように行動し、発話し、他者に耳を傾け、その場の関係と言説を形成するのか、そのパフォーマティビティに光を当てる。そこに自己と社会の枠組みや関係を捉え直す可能性を追求する自らの芸術的実践について、ファン・オルデンボルフは次のように述べている。「(私の実践は)何かを思考し、知覚し、解釈し、認識し、構築することにおいて、オルタナティブな編成を見つけ、形づくることにある。この実践は決してひとつのフォーマットや方法に固定されることはなく、その時々の状況に応じて常に変化する[1]。」

本展タイトル「柔らかな舞台」は、私とファン・オルデンボルフが付けた「unset on-set」という英語のタイトルを意訳したもので、上述した彼女の実践のプロセスと作用を示唆しつつ、この展覧会のために制作した、映像の内と外の身体、視線、声が交差する舞台（セット）のようなインスタレーションを指すものでもある。そこで展示した《マウリッツ・スクリプト》《偽りなき響き》（二〇〇八年）《彼女たちの》（二〇一九年）、《ヒア》（二〇二一年）《オブサダ》（二〇二一年）、そして新作である《ふたつの石》（二〇二二年）は、ファン・オルデンボルフがこれまでに継続的に取り組んできた植民地主義、ナショナリズム、家父長制、ジェンダーといった問題領域を取り上げる。多くの既存作品からこれらの選定に至るまでには、遠く離れつつも繋がり合っている私たちの歴史と社会において、上述の問題がいかに交差し、影響し合っているかについての長い対話があり、それが日本の文脈に対するファン・オルデンボルフの関心や、新たな作品を制作するモチベーションを喚起することとなった。

私とファン・オルデンボルフがオンラインで定期的な話し合いを始めたのは二〇二一年の春、彼女がオランダで《ヒア》を発表し、ポーランドでの《オブサダ》の撮影を準備していた時期であった。これらの作品では、女性の文化生産者や研究者たちが、音楽や詩や対話を通じて自らのアイデンティティと内に抱えた脆弱性を問い直し、自己の主観性を表現する言語を共に模索する。「新たな声はすでにそこにある」と言うファン・オルデンボルフにとって、それは規範や言説、あるいは言葉そのものに内在する権力構造から自己を解放する隙間を押し広げる声である。

1
Wendelien van Oldenborgh,
"The Work We Do," Amateur (Berlin:
Sternberg Press; London: The
Showroom, 2014), 373.

　　　　　　　　崔 敬華

二〇二二年の秋に東京と横浜で撮影された《彼女たちの》では、社会に置かれた自らの位置に抗う女性たちの声が現在と過去を跨り、共鳴する。世代、国籍、ジェンダーや職業も異なる十一人のキャストが、太平洋戦争前後の時代を作家として生き抜いた林芙美子と宮本百合子による断片を読み上げる。そして率直に、互いに思慮深く、自らの経験や推論から、生の理想も政治的姿勢もかけ離れていた林と宮本それぞれにとっての抵抗や切望を文脈付け、彼女たちに対する共感、異議、解釈の迷いを表明する。二人の文章の異なる主題と文体、そして言語（日本語と英語）を行き来するキャストの間には、共鳴や微妙な不協和といった間主体的な力学が立ち現れる。時間と空間の実験を折り重ねるかのごとく、動き続ける二つのフレームを組み合わせたファン・オルデンボルフの視覚的な実験にも示唆されているように、この断片的な会話のアッサンブラージュからは、文章／語り手と、それを読むキャスト／聞き手の間、そして他の聞き手に語りかける語り手としてのキャストの間に差異が生成され続ける。それは、差異が常に倫理的、政治的な交渉に開かれていることを示唆しつつ、知り得ないこと、翻訳し得ないこととどのように折り合いをつけるのか、あるいは他者との距離をどのようにして近さあるいは遠さとして認識するのかといった、個々に託された行為者性を問う。ファン・オルデンボルフはこのように、自己と、そのあらゆるものとの関係を捉え、また捉え直すための流動的なトポスに私たちを招き入れる。

最後に、多大な熱意をもって本展の制作に取り組み、三ヶ月という長くも短い期間、東京に滞在し新作に挑んでくれたファン・オルデンボルフ氏をはじめ、彼女との協働に労を惜しまなかったキャストとクルー、そして洞察に富んだ文章を本書に寄せてくれた菅野優香氏、ビンナ・チョイ氏、パブロ・デ・オカンポ氏と、素晴らしいインタビューをしてくれたアンドリュー・マークル氏に深い感謝の意を表する。

不透明なフェミニスト／クィア・ポリフォニー

菅野優香

語ること、そして語り合うことがその映像世界をかたち作る主要な営為としてあるウェンデリン・ファン・オルデンボルフの作品は、しばしば「ポリフォニー」によって特徴づけられてきた。もともとは多声音楽を意味するこの概念をドストエフスキーの詩学の原理として見出したのはミハエル・バフチンであったが、文学理論としてまた芸術思想として再概念化されたポリフォニーとは、作者と登場人物が対話をし、複数の声がその自律性を保ちながら鳴り響く「開かれた」空間を可能にするものである。だが、ファン・オルデンボルフ的なポリフォニーを紐解くためのもうひとつの重要な視座がフェミニズムであろう。というのも、複数の声を聞きながら、共存する多数の読みの可能性を拓いてきた批評的実践こそがフェミニズムだからである。統一的であることに抵抗し、分裂や矛盾を恐れることなく、むしろそうした一貫性の欠如に意義を見出し、両義的であることに価値を置くフェミニスト批評は、ことばやイメージの意味が横滑りし、脱線し、多元化されるところに、女性たちの葛藤や緊張関係を読み解く試みである。

ファン・オルデンボルフのフェミニスト的ポリフォニーを支えるスタイルと美学の中心にあるのが、移動と断片性、そして不透明さである。絶えずゆっくりと移動するカメラの運動によって、ゆるやかに変化し続ける視点と、唐突に流れを切断し、滑らかさを拒むかのようにつながれる断片的なショット。物質性を剥き出しにしながら、表面へと視線を導く不透明なイメージは、視覚を通さない厚みを持つ。文字通り「動きで書く」シネマトグラフィーと、ショットの自律性を強調し断片化する編集とともに現れるこの不透明なイメージこそは、明晰さや連続性、可視性から遠ざかるファン・オルデンボルフ的映像世界の要所である。

新作となる《彼女たちの》（二〇二二年）は、近代日本の女性文学者たちを素材として構想されているが、

25

菅野優香

この試みは、《ふたつの石》（二〇一九年）、《ヒア》（二〇二二年）、《オブサダ》（二〇二二年）といった今回展示される作品はもちろんのこと、《ベテ＆デイズ》（二〇一二年）といった中期の作品にも通底する〈女性たちの関係〉に対する関心と響き合うものだ。これまでのファン・オルデンボルフの映像世界を作り上げてきたテクストを読むという行為が、《彼女たちの》においても反復される。登場人物たちが声だけでなく、さまざまな身振りや姿勢という身体性をもってテクストを朗読するとき、過去と現在が接触し、歴史に沈澱していた意味が新たな意味となって現代に浮上する。

例えば、《ふたつの石》で交差するテクストは、活動家であるヘルミナ・ハウスヴァウトによる文章と、建築家ロッテ・スタム゠ベーゼが関わった都市計画や公共住宅計画の記憶を継承した場所や建物である。《彼女たちの》でも同様だが、ファン・オルデンボルフの作品にあっては、文章だけでなく、場所や建物もまたテクストとなる。さまざまなアングルとフレーミングによって多角的に捉えられた都市や建物の記憶が、現在に生きる人物の多様な「声」によって呼び起こされ、むくりと起き上がってくる。テクストとテクストが触れ合い、互いの境界を侵犯し混じり合うとき、交差する複数のテクストはその多層性と多声性によっ

て不透明なものとなる。

《ヒア》では、書かれたものや音楽を含めた複数のメディウムによって構成されるテクストが触れ合い、共鳴し合う。だが、そこで生じている複数のテクストの交差は、ゆるやかな動きとともにもたらされはするものの、決して滑らかに連続しているわけではない。帰属やセクシュアリティについて語るそれらのテクストは、中断したり、停滞したり、突如加速するリズムの不規則性によって明瞭な目的を欠いたまま、

さまざまな女性たちによって読まれていく。これらが生起する場所が改装中の美術館であることは重要である。建物の構造や素材の細部にいたるまで、カメラはあますことなくその物質性を視覚化していくが、それは過去と現在の接触を可能にするファン・オルデンボルフ的空間である。

女性であることによって生じる経験の固有性を、そして女性間の関係性を、それらの差異を決して消し去ることなく探求する《彼女たちの》は、《ベテ＆デイズ》が意図せず露呈させたフェミニスト的ポリフォニーの変奏となっているように思われる。《ベテ＆デイズ》に登場する二人の女性の邂逅は、政治性の意味を再審し、政治的であることの意味と可能性を押し拡げる。女優のベテ・メンデスは、ブラジル国内のさまざまな政治活動に携わってきた人物であり、一般的な意味において政治的な女性である。歌手のデイズ・ティグロナは、政治を語る既存の用語に頼ることがなく、一見非政治的な人物であるが、女性をエンパワーするその歌詞やパフォーマンスによって、意図せざる政治性を生み出している。対話する二人の関係は、友好的なものから不穏なものへと変化していくが、その関係性に生じるズレやひびをこの作品は丁寧に描き出していく。階級と人種の異なる二人の女性が生み出す「政治的であること」の多様性は、女性というカテゴリーの雑種性を逆照射し、その可能性を拡張する。

ファン・オルデンボルフの映像世界において前景化される女同士の関係は、ときに「絆」や「連帯」を示唆しつつも、それらによって完全には包摂されえない複雑で矛盾に満ちた情動的なつながりを示している。《彼女たちの》で取り上げられている三人の女性たちにも、女性であることの固有の経験によって生み出される差異がくっきりと刻み込まれている。と同時に、女性というアイデンティティの不安定さと不

透明さは、女性であることの意味を作り直す契機となる。詩人として出発した後、『放浪記』や『浮雲』といった作品で昭和を代表する女性作家となった林芙美子。十八歳のとき『貧しき人々の群』で文壇にデビューし、後にプロレタリア文学のパイオニアとなった宮本百合子。雑誌記者からロシア文学の翻訳者となった湯浅芳子。文学との関わり方も、出自も異なる三人の女性が召喚され、ファン・オルデンボルフの映像世界で邂逅を果たす。

林芙美子という文学的磁場

林芙美子はなぜこんなにも他の女性作家たちを呼び寄せるのだろうか。同時代に生きた平林たい子による評伝をはじめ、今日でも多くの女性作家が林芙美子という文学的磁場に引き寄せられている。現代の日本社会で女性の抱える困難を最も鋭く抉り続けてきた作家・桐野夏生は、創作と史実が入り混じった林芙美子のモデル小説『ナニカアル』を書き、「南方で何があったのか」を再想像する。ジェンダーとセクシュアリティの規範性を問い直しながら女性の性愛や女性同士の関係について実験的な小説を発表してきた松浦理英子もまた『裏ヴァージョン』で林芙美子を喚起する。二人の女性のクィアな関係を描くこの小説には、短編小説の書き手である昌子が登場するが、彼女が「挫折する作家として過去を語る」この作品は、飯田祐子に従えば、『放浪記』のパロディである。批評的距離をもとにした転倒と反復をパロディとするならば、『裏ヴァージョン』は『放浪記』に対して、女性として小説を書くこと、あるいは、書く主

1 佐久間文子は『ナニカアル』が、林の最高傑作とされる『浮雲』の創作の謎に迫るべく書かれたのではないかと推測している。佐久間文子「解説」、桐野夏生『ナニカアル』所収、新潮文庫、二〇一二年、五八五頁。

体としての女が自らの経験を題材とする「自伝的」な小説を、誰にどのように語るかに意識的であることによって批評的距離を保っているのだ。そして、『放浪記』の自伝的性質とは、それが事実か虚構かではなく、林個人の体験を超えた社会的主体としての女のあり方を執拗に問う点にある。『放浪記』を「増築に増築を重ねた、奇怪な建造物」と呼ぶ小平麻衣子は、この小説が自伝的であるのは、それが事実に立脚しているからではなく、女性を取り巻く状況との長年の交渉を織り込んでいるからだと述べる。③

死ぬまで『放浪記』をアップデートし続けた林の書く主体への意志は、「女であること」の強烈な自己意識にも貫かれているが、そこでは自らの性が抜き差しならないかたちで社会と接続されている。現代の日本に生きる女性作家たちは、女の位置をめぐる林の逡巡に応答し、その格闘を自らのサバイバルと重ね合わせているかのようである。そして今、《彼女たちの》とともに、私たちは再び林芙美子の読者になろうとしている。そこで出会い直す林芙美子とは、帝国主義が膨張させた日本の幻影を「男女の状況」に置き換えて表現しただけではない。クィアな眼差しと欲望を他の女性に向け、クィアな可能性に満ちた女同士の関係を、個人の欲望としてだけでなく、社会的主体としての女の生成の条件に含めた林芙美子なのである。④ きわめて直裁に「性」を語った林は、その射程を必ずしも異性愛に限定したわけではないことが本展示で明らかになる。

2 高校時代の友人であった二人の女性のやりとりからなるこの小説は、ひとりの書いた短編小説と、それに対する厳しいコメントからなる十八の章によって構成されており、今は中年となった二人のクィアな関係を軸に展開される。飯田祐子「彼女たちの文学――語りにくさと読まれること」、名古屋大学出版会、二〇一六年。

3 小平麻衣子「林芙美子・〈赤裸々〉の匙かげん――『放浪記』の書きかえをめぐって――」『早稲田文学増刊 女性号』一〇二六号（筑摩書房刊 二〇一七年）、四〇二頁。

4 例えば坂元さおりは、現在の研究史において『浮雲』が林の最高到達点とされる理由として「登場人物たちが『拡大／縮小する日本』の波打ち際に放り出され、そこで起こるダイナミズムが具体的な男女の状況に置換されて表現されている」点を挙げている。坂元さおり「『ナニカアル』の〈傷跡〉――戦争／植民の『記憶』と『記録』」『思想』一一五九号（岩波書店、二〇二〇年）、四九頁。

移動すること

　林芙美子、宮本百合子、湯浅芳子の数少ない共通点のひとつが「移動」である。そして、この移動は地理的な転移(ディスロケーション)を意味するだけでなく、社会的で心的なものである。放浪という名の移動から書く主体としての女を立ち上げた林は、『放浪記』の冒頭で、「私は宿命的に放浪者である。私は古里を持たない」と記したが、この小説で流行作家となってからも、林は移動し続けた。朝鮮、シベリア、フランス、イギリスへの旅をはじめ、日中戦争が始まると陥落した南京に「女流作家」として一番乗りし、その後は従軍作家として漢口に従軍した体験を『戦線』や『北岸部隊』などに書き綴った。その後、南方に徴用されて視察した、シンガポール、マレー半島、ボルネオは、後の作品の重要な舞台となっている。最後の作品となった『浮雲』もまた、放浪する女の物語であった[5]。『放浪記』と『浮雲』にあって、とりわけ重要公の女性たちは、林自身の移動を反復し、移動の意味を重層化する。例えば『放浪記』におなのが、女としての「私」が移動することの意味である。戦前、いて重要なのは、女の「位置」からはずれていくという意味での移動である。戦中、戦後にわたり(そしておそらく現在でもそう事情は変わらないが)、女が帰属すべき場所、あるいは女が女としての位置を割り当てられてきたのは、二つの家である。生まれ育った家と、妻や母としての役割を担う家である。この二つの家を離れることによって、「女」から離脱していく「私」を描く『放浪記』の移動は、自由と不安、解放と貧困の間を往還する両義的なものである。放浪とは、明らかにジェンダー化されており、女性が移動することと男性が移動することの意味はあまりに大きく異なっている。さらに『放浪記』の移動とは、複数の男性

5　一九五一年、林が亡くなった直後に出版された『めし』は、朝日新聞に連載中かつ三分の二を書き上げたばかりであったため、実際には未完の小説である。

の間を放浪する「私」が、ときに異性愛的欲望からも逸脱する際にも生じるものだ。

　プロレタリア文学のパイオニアである宮本百合子も移動には事欠かなかった。十九歳でコロンビア大学（ニューヨーク）の聴講生となった宮本は、パリ、ロンドンなど、裕福な教育一家に育った「才媛」らしい旅の人生を送った。だが、ロシア文学の翻訳者であった湯浅芳子との親密な関係は、宮本にとって言わばセクシュアリティをめぐる移動でもあったろう。夫と別れて湯浅と生活をともにし、その後また男性との関係に入っていった宮本は、セクシュアリティの移動者、往還者でもあった。もちろんその軌跡は行ったり来たりを繰り返す蛇行のようなものであり、湯浅との関係の後、宮本が女性との性愛や官能を伴う親密な関係に入っていくことは二度となかった。二人の間で交わされた手紙には、セクシュアリティの移動者となることの宮本の不安と躊躇いとともに、女性同性愛者を自認していた湯浅にとってもまた宮本を愛することの葛藤がまざまざと刻まれている。[6] 引っ越し魔として知られた湯浅も国内の住処を転々としたが、百合子と芳子はともに過ごした七年間、移動し続けた。シベリア鉄道で釜山を経由しモスクワに着いた二人はソビエトに三年ほど滞在したが、その間、ワルシャワ、ウィーン、ベルリン、パリなどを旅している。

　移動し続けた彼女たちと行動をともにしたのがY・Y・Cというネーム入りの黒いトランクであった。「愛は、二人で提げてゆく包みのようなもの」と記した湯浅のことばを引きつつ、二人の往復書簡を整理し、その意味を考察した文学者の黒澤亜里子は、この黒いトランクに入っていたのは「愛と友情」という不思議な夢の気体であると言う。だが、中身を透視させない黒いトランクは、まさに二人の関係を物質化したもののようである。芳子に対する自らの激し

6　宮本との出会いから別れまでに焦点を当てた湯浅の優れた評伝として以下のものがある。沢部仁美『百合子、ダスヴィダーニヤ―湯浅芳子の青春』文藝春秋、一九九〇年。

菅野優香

い感情を「衝動」と呼びつつも、恋愛や性愛、官能は異性との間でのみ生じるという考えから抜け切るこ
とができず、二人の関係を「友愛」と規定しようとした宮本と、自らの女性に対する感情を「愛」と認め
ながらも、女同士の愛は不可能だと考えていた湯浅。二人の関係性は、どこまでいっても黒いトランクの
ように不透明なまま動き続けた。黒澤は、宮本と湯浅の間で交わされた手紙を優れた恋愛文学のテクスト
と呼び、そこに「多数の強度、可変的な色彩、見えにくい動き、移りやすい形態」（フーコー）を持った
多様な関係のヴァリエーションを見出している。そして、往復書簡のうちに、「ありふれた日常の中に存
在している無数の可能性のひとつ」を読み取った黒澤もまた、《彼女たちの》の登場人物として、女同士
の関係を語る「声」となる。人種、年齢、ジェンダーやセクシュアリティの異なる登場人物たちが、林の
小説、宮本の作品、宮本と湯浅の往復書簡を朗読するとき、彼女たちの身体と記憶、感情や知が刻印され
た声の集積が不規則に反響する。その断片化された不透明なフェミニスト／クィア・ポリフォニーは、作
品の中を、そして作品を超えて移動し続ける。

7
黒澤亜里子編著『往復書簡
宮本百合子と湯浅芳子』翰林書房、
二〇〇八年、六頁。

菅野優香（かんの・ゆうか）
同志社大学大学院グローバル・スタディーズ研究科准教授。専門分野は、映画・視覚文化研究、クィア・スタディーズ。映像におけるジェンダーやセクシュアリティ、人種の問題に関心を寄せ、クィア・シネマや映画祭をテーマに、映像とアクティビズム、コミュニティの生成などの問題に取り組んでいる。編著『クィア・シネマ・スタディーズ』（晃洋書房、二〇二一年）、共著に『Routledge Handbook of Japanese Cinema』(Routledge、二〇二一年)『The Japanese Cinema Book』(Bloomsbury Academic、二〇二〇年)『クィア・スタディーズをひらく』（晃洋書房、二〇二〇年）『ジェンダーと生政治〈戦後日本を読みかえる〉』（臨川書店、二〇一九年）『川島雄三は二度生まれる』（水声社、二〇一八年）など。

菅野優香

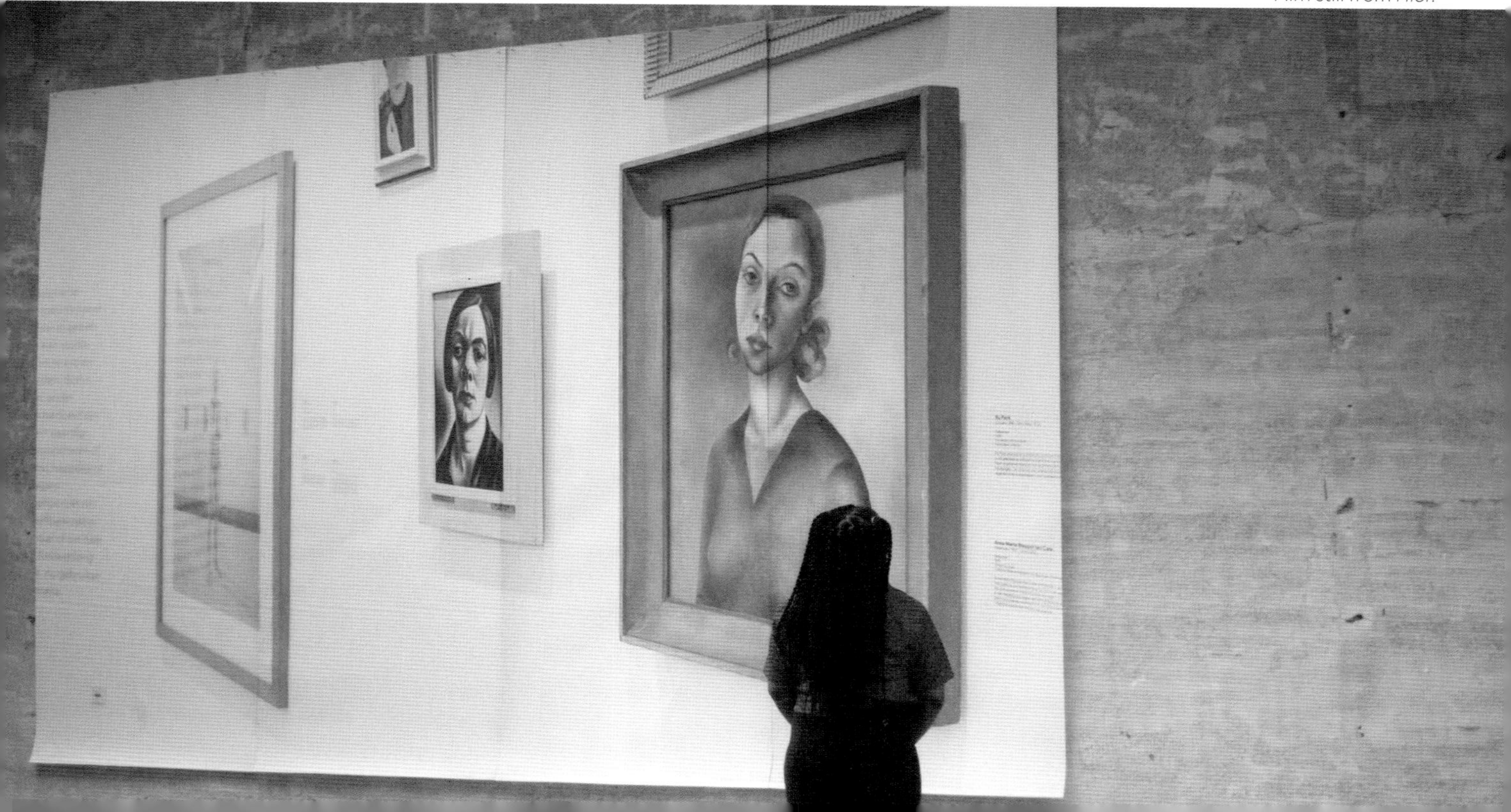

《ヒア》映像スチル

Film still from *Hier*.

〈ふたつの石〉映像スチル

Film still from *Two Stones*

《偽りなき響き》撮影記録　撮影：エミリアーノ・ガンドルフィ

Production still from No False Echoes, photo by Emiliano Gandolfi

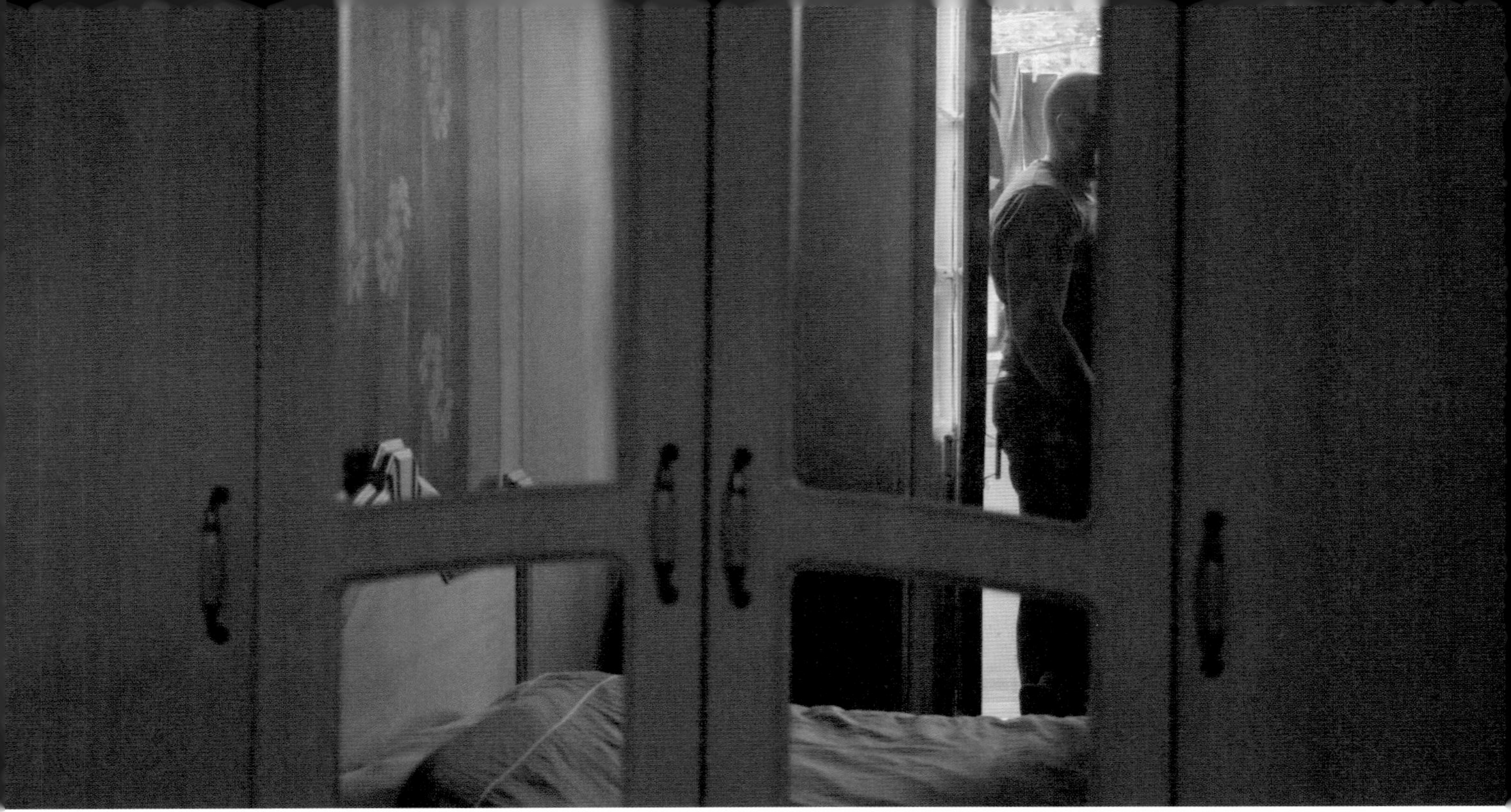

《ふたつの石》映像スチル

Film still from *Two Stones*

《ヒア》映像スチル

Film still from Hier.

〈ふたつの石〉映像スチル

Film still from *Two Stones*

《オブサダ》撮影記録　撮影：ヤコブ・ダニレヴィッチ

Production still from obsada, photo by Jakub Danilewicz

〈ふたつの石〉映像スチル

Film still from *Two Stones*

我々が集う時

ビンナ・チョイ

片桐由賀　訳

私は最近、オランダの今後数年間の文化政策に対し市民の意見を聴く公聴会に聴衆として参加するために、オランダの国会を訪れる機会を得た。一日がかりで行われる公聴会は、テーマ別のセッションで構成されており、各セッションでは、文化芸術各分野の代表者が数分ずつ発言した後に国会議員からの質問が行われる。この日は一日中一般の人が見学できたが、質問や議論への参加は禁止されていた（このルールについて特に指示はなかったが、公聴会の仕組みと進行の仕方からわかるようになっていた）。高度に演出された節度ある振る舞いによって、全てがスムーズに進行していく。招待された参加者全員に均等な時間枠が与えられ、控えめではないが礼儀正しく、芝居がかることなく改まった話し方で、誰もが行儀よく発言している。この環境においては、最先端の個別マイクや音響に配慮した内装など、入念に準備された会議をサポートするための仕組みが重要な役割を担っていた。まるで演技をしているかのように飲み物を提供する男性もこれに含まれており、彼の小道具のように見えるグラスの入った引き戸のキャビネットも、会の妨げにならないようにスムーズに機能していた。こうしてスピーチは続いた。これはいわゆる民主主義的な制度の空間であり、この空間ではさまざまな意見が聴かれることになっている。つまり、言葉のやりとりが行われていることに他ならない。

どういうわけかこの議会制の時空は、私にウェンデリン・ファン・オルデンボルフの映像作品の時空を思い起こさせた。彼女の作品の多くには、建築、歴史、政治といった観点から特別な重要性を持つ場所に「演者＝参加者」の一団が集合する。作品の内容やテーマと特別な関係にあることを理由に作家から招待された人々の多くは、その関係を言葉で表現し、議論し、常に互いを尊重しつつも時に討論に至る。彼女の作品のテーマは、挑発的とまではいかないまでも時事的であり、特定の国や地域の文脈に見られる世論に触

れつつ、より幅広い意味合いを含んでいる。また、作品に登場する人たち全員が語りながらも、誰もが雄弁であると同時に優雅に見えることも特筆すべき点である。また、観客でないとすれば無言の目撃者として作品に登場する「観客＝参加者」も同様である。彼女の作品は、必ずしも直接的な意見の一致を求めるものではないが、多様性が成功要因になる傾向がある。彼女の作品は、多様な立場や知識に耳を傾け、そ
れについて話し、議論するための空間を作り出すのである。この体験から私は「それは、ファン・オルデンボルフの作品が民主的な解釈の実践であることを示唆しているのだろうか？」と自問するようになった。

もちろん、議会制の民主的な空間とファン・オルデンボルフの映画的な集いの空間の比較には、研究と検証が必要になるだろう。この二つの形式がどのようにして互いを映し合っているのかを単純に列挙していくと、反動的に見えてしまう恐れがある。このことは、代表制民主主義とその制度的な空間において想定されるコミュニケーションの調和的機能の肯定を招くが、これが誤りであることは周知の事実である。むしろその研究においては、この二つが実際に互いにどう異なっているのか、その間に横たわる距離は何を表しているのかを掘り下げるべきである。本稿は、そのような研究の端緒を開くことを意図しており、そ
の一環として《偽りなき響き》（二〇〇八年）に焦点を当てる。この映像作品は、題材と手法の両面において、二〇〇五年以降にこの作家が制作した作品の典型的な特徴を示しているだけでなく、オランダの民主主義体制を支える「柱」を揺るがした出来事、続く反民主主義的な政治勢力の台頭とそれに伴う文化的転回とも時期を同じくしている。

ブリコラージュ

二〇〇八年は世界的な金融危機が始まった年だが、オランダではまだ顕在化していなかった。国粋主義及びポピュリズム政治の台頭の引き金となった未曾有の政治的事件の余波に揺れるオランダでは、金融危機ではなく、多文化主義やイスラム嫌悪に関する言説が支配的だった。二〇〇二年には、ピム・フォルタイン党（LPF）を設立したピム・フォルタインが総選挙中に暗殺される。それは彼が、反イスラム・反移民の立場を、歯に衣着せないカリスマ的とも言える口調で語り、急速に人気を集めていた時期に起こった。それからわずか二年後、政治的暗殺が再び起こる。今度の標的は、イスラム文化や多文化主義を露骨に批判し、挑発と論争を好んだ映画監督でコラムニストのテオ・ファン・ゴッホだった。最初の事件の犯人がオランダ人の環境保護・動物愛護活動家（フォルカー・ファン・デル・フラーフ）であったのに対し、ファン・ゴッホを殺したのがモロッコ系オランダ市民の青年（モハンマド・ブウィエリ）だったことにより、国粋主義者、さらには人種差別主義者による抗議が激化する。これを受けたオランダの文化政策は、当時盛んに唱えられていた、オランダ社会に新たに顕在化した緊張と不安定化に対する政治的及び一般的な分析に沿う形で、多文化主義を重点的に取り上げるようになったのである。このことは、あらゆる芸術文化施設のプログラムに目に見える形で影響を及ぼすことになった。ファン・アッベ美術館の多面的なプロジェクト「Be[com]ing Dutch」もその一例である。これにより、同館はモンドリアン財団から「文化的多様性開発賞」を受賞している。このプロジェクトを通じて、展覧会はもちろん、討論会、読書会、さまざまな機関による全国規模のコラボレーションなど、幅広いプログラムが二年間（二〇〇七—二〇〇八年）にわたって展開された。《偽りなき響き》はこのような背景において制作されている。同美術館からの依頼を

我々が集う時　　46

受けた作家の応答は、新たな挑発や一方的なイデオロギー的立場の安易な表明をするのではなく、最近の政治的な出来事を深掘りするものであった。そうする代わりに、彼女はさまざまな背景を持つ多数の人々を招待し、複雑に絡み合った一連の物語に我々の注意を向けさせる。こうして、ひとつの集いが行われるのである。

しかし、この集いは典型的なものではない。彼女が招いた人々は、言うなれば国会に出席するような人々が属しているのと同じ専門的な仕事や組織の枠組みには属さない（たとえば、私が出席した公聴会では、さまざまな文化施設の館長が文化芸術の幅広い分野を代表して発言していた）。そして、彼らはまるで議会の出席者のように、自分たちが所属する団体の代表として決められた立場から発言しているわけでもない。我々が目にするのは、映画のためのリサーチあるいは偶然の出会いを通じて作家自身が知り合った、ラッパー、ラジオプロデューサー、学者、編集者などである。集会が行われる建物の中やその周辺のあちこちで、座ったり立ったりしているのはそういう人たちである。では、彼らをよく見てみよう。

作品の大部分で建物のバルコニーに立っているのは、モロッコ系オランダ人の人気ラッパー、サラ・エディーンだ。この作品に出演する直前には、（フォルタインのように）反イスラム・反移民の姿勢で物議を醸している政治家、ヘルト・ウィルダースの映画で彼の写真が使われている。その映画は、エディーンを暗殺者モハンマド・ボウィェリに見せかけることによって、人種差別の眼差しがどのように機能するかを明らかにしていた。[1] エディーンの歌詞は社会政治的な批判を特徴とし、「この…の国」（Het Land

1 エディーンのアルバム『オランダの最悪の悪夢』（Nederlands Grootste Nachtmerrie）の表紙写真には、この眼差しをあざ笑うかのように、ボウィェリそっくりのエディーンの写真が使われている。

　　　　　　　　　ビンナ・チョイ

Van...）という曲で表現したように、イスラムを嫌悪するオランダ社会に対する痛烈な批判が込められている。この作品の中でエディーンは、自分の歌詞をラップするのではなく、インドネシアの民族主義者スワルディ・スルヤニングラットが一九一三年に発表した記事「もし私がオランダ人であったなら」（"Als ik eens Nederlander was"）を朗読している。この文章は、オランダの植民地支配を雄弁に批判し、インドネシアの独立と自由の必要性を強く喚起するものだ。この作品では、このテキストを精一杯読み上げながら演じるエディーンを中心に、リハーサルや失敗の瞬間も見ることができる。エディーンは自分自身として、あるいは自分自身を演じながら、別の時代にオランダ政権へ敵対する立場をとった歴史的人物であるスルヤニングラットを体現しようと試みる。一方、それ以外の人々は、建物内の高い位置にある中二階でまとまって座ったり、立ったりしている。ラジオプロデューサーのウィム・ノルドフックは、自身のラジオ番組「De Avonden」について語っている。彼は二〇〇二から二〇〇四年にかけて、この番組でオランダ・インドネシア植民地時代のラジオ放送から選りすぐったアーカイブを放送していた。オランダ・フィリップス社が自社の送信機を使って一九二〇年代に開始したこれらの歴史的な番組は、インドネシア（旧オランダ領東インド）に住むオランダ人とインドネシア人の富裕層の両方に向けて発信されていた。ノルドフックだけでなく、インドネシア研究者で『独白から対話へ：インドネシアのラジオと改革』（*From Monologue to Dialogue: Radio and Reform in Indonesia, 2009*）の著者であるエドウィン・ユリエンスも示しているように、ラジオ放送は近代化のプロセスに貢献し、ヨーロッパのライフスタイルをインドネシア人にとって身近なものにした。これらの番組は、ダンス音楽、心の悩みに対するアドバイス、娯楽といった「軽い」コンテンツに的を絞り、政治的プロパガンダは一切放送していない。テレビ以前の時代、そしてYouTube以前の時代にラジオは、植民地の風景を支配するメディアとして機能していたのだろう。しか

し、フェミニスト哲学者であり、文化的多様性研究者であるバウキェ・プリンスは、この歴史の別の側面に光を当てている。入植者の国だった一九二〇年代のオランダでは、いわゆる「セクト主義」あるいは「柱状社会[i]」と呼ばれる状態、つまり、対立や交渉の必要性を減らすために互いに分離したままの状態を保つことによって異なる思想や宗教を持つ共同体が共存するための合意が成立していた。そしてこれは世俗的、自由主義的、人文主義的なオランダ人の共同体が、反革命的で保守的な政党に譲歩するという代償の上に成り立っていた。

《偽りなき響き》に見られるような集まりを位置付けるとするならば、「民主的多元主義の一形態」という表現がもっとも適切かもしれない。もしそうだとすれば、これはまだ現実には存在しないものなのかもしれない。これを明確に言い表しているものの一例として、ホミ・K・バーバが説くブリコラージュの概念が挙げられる。

（ブリコラージュによって）ひとつの伝統、あるいはさまざまな思考の伝統に共感しつつ、これは古くてこれは新しいというような、ある種の時間的・概念的な無責任さに陥ることなく、異なるもの、オリジナルなもの、際立ったものを明確に表現できるようになる[2]。

訳註 i　宗派別あるいはイデオロギー別に分離した社会を、オランダ語で「柱 (verzuiling)」と言い、「柱状社会」と訳すことができる。ひとつの分割された縦割り構造の社会を「柱」と表現している。

2　ソランジュ・デ・ボーアとゾーイ・グレイによるホミ・K・バーバへのインタビュー。Source Book t. Brian Jungen (Rotterdam: Witte de With, 2006), 24.

　　　　　　　　　　ビンナ・チョイ

さらにバーバは「ブリコラージュには全体性や境界がない」とも述べている。ブリコラージュとは、我々が立っている不確かな地面のことであり、ひとつの問題を均質なあるいは分離可能ないくつもの問題に分解するのではなく、型にはまらない思考の軌跡や動きを可能にする、特別で一時的な事実に向かわせる。

さらにバーバが、ブリコルール（ブリコラージュをする人）は「過去の呪縛や亡霊がドアの外に追い出されることはありえないと感じている」と言う時、私は、ファン・オルデンボルフの作品で起きているのはブリコラージュであり、ファン・オルデンボルフはブリコルールであると確信する。

この集いの見えない主催者である作家は、反植民地闘争／独立運動といった未解決の過去や同時代のオランダの社会変化の断片に加え、技術発展の歴史やメディアの風景もブリコラージュし、今世紀に入ってからオランダ社会、そして西洋社会全般がそれにとっての「他者」に関連して経験してきた過渡期とそれ・ら・の・も・つ・れ・を探究している。バーバは、ブリコラージュの実践によって、「移行につきもの・の・一・次・性・を持続させることができる（傍点筆者）」と述べている。何が起こるかわからないからこそ、あなたは到達手段としての過渡期の偶発的な経路に積極的に関わるのだ。ブリコラージュ＝集いは、民主主義や芸術において未知に向かって移行するための手段として、現代にふさわしい形式かもしれない。それは、昔より今の方がやらなければならないことがたくさんあり、過去と未来の全ての重荷に加えて我々自身もまたその一部である可能性を示している。

3　前掲書。

研究会

この作品の中で、集まった人たちは皆、自分の書いたテキストに加え、現在と過去の他人の書いたテキストを読む。これは台本を暗記して読むのとは異なり、演技の影に読むという行為が隠れていることもない。むしろ、言葉を発する人たちが、朗読、テキストを演じる、独白という非活動的な表現形式の間を行き来することにより、演技とは何であって何でないのか、自分の意見とは何であって何でないのか、どこまでが過去の話でどこからが現在の話なのかが曖昧になっている。この曖昧な状況は、一体何を作り出そうとしているのだろうか。歴史的及び現代的な政治・社会的情報を満載したこれらの断片の朗読は、沈黙したままの我々が読むことをどのようにして可能にするのか。このことから、どのような統一的見解や政治的プロセスを作り出すことができるのだろう。研究会、それが私の答えだ。

一部の人にとって、研究とは学術研究から派生した概念かもしれない。研究とは、誰かの指導のもとに自律性を欠いた状態で行う行為である。しかし、フレッド・モートンとステファノ・ハーニーが提唱するように、研究とは教室や講義室だけではなく、「一種のワークショップに参加する、バンドで演奏する、ジャムセッションをする、あるいはポーチに座っている老人、工場で一緒に働いている人[4]」といった状況下で、同じように苦労する人々の間ですでに起きている、思弁的な実践でもあるのだ。今日の学術研究は、多くの大学で見られるように、企業の利益のために利用され、

4
「Studying through the Undercommons: Stefano Harney and Fred Moten Interviewed by Stevphen Shukaitis」を参照。Class War University, 二〇一二年十一月十二日、http://classwaru.org/2012/11/12/studying-through-the-undercommons-stefano-harney-fred-moten-interviewed-by-stevphen-shukaitis/。

51　　　ビンナ・チョイ

5 このエッセイでは焦点を当てていないが、作家の別の映像作品、《Instruction》（二〇〇九年）にも、この研究という概念が登場し、さらに例証されていることについて考えることは有意義だろう。この作品では、オランダ国防大学を舞台に、若い士官候補生たちがテキストを読み、一九四〇年代後半にインドネシアの独立軍に対して行われたオランダ軍の介入について議論する。指示あるいは命令で規律でありながら、倫理的・政治的区別がつかないような状況における自分たちの行動の倫理的範囲について、士官候補生たちは熟考し、共に研究する。

管理階級に支配されているが、皮肉なことに、教師も学生も未だに自分たちを労働者とは異なる存在だと考えている。モートンとハーニーは、制度化、資本化、植民地化という目的でそのような形の研究を支配・抑圧するものに対抗して人々が互いに関連している限り、研究とはむしろ、労働者やいわゆる知識人、それどころかあらゆる人の「一般的な知的実践」であると論じているのだ。

《偽りなき響き》で起きている、異なる時代や文化を超えた立場、思想、概念のブリコラージュ作業は、研究の一形態と考えてよいだろう。(s) それぞれの朗読は別の朗読に敏感に反応し、会話と思索的な「フューチャリング」(ii) を導きながら、見る者にある種の研究様式に入り込むきっかけを与える。

訳注ii 「フューチャリング (Futuring)」とは、未来について考え、可能性のある結果を想像し、未来を計画するための体系的なプロセスに関する学問である。

ファン・オルデンボルフの作品においては、一見平和で民主的なオランダ社会に何が起きたのか、忘れられたものや考えられなかったものがどのようにして現状を解明しているのか、あるいはこうした過去の断片から我々は何を学ぶことができるのか、社会的・政治的環境においてメディアや「新しい」テクノロジーがどのようにして効果/作用を生み出しているのか、といったさまざまな問いについて、話者と（作品内外の）観客が等しく研究し、熟考することが求められる。もしオランダの民主主義体制が、柱状化の代わりに意見の相違や紛争に対処する別の方法を見出していたら、社会がイスラム教徒に偏見を持つ人や移民などに分断されている現在の対立的な状況を回避できたのだろうか。バウキェ・プリンスはそう考えているようで、フェミニストの思考

訳注iii サブカルチャーを中心に組織化された「柱」が社会を分節化することを「柱状化」という。

様式と「インターセクショナリズム(iv)」の実践という観点からこれを説明している。

それとも、今のメディアの「言論の自由」に対する敏感さは、インドネシアのスハルト独裁政権下でのメディアの独占と類似しているのか。後者に関するエドウィン・ユリエンスの物語は、そうであることを暗示しているかもしれないが、「今日のメディアを支配し、運営し、金を出しているのは誰?」「ヒップホップをはじめとする大衆文化の影響は?」といった他のさまざまな声によって複雑化されている。無限のブリコラージュには、無限の研究がつきまとう。

モートンとハーニーの研究の概念は、資本主義的な行動を象徴する計画や物流の方法と対照をなすジャズの即興演奏の経験にも依拠している。この即興演奏は、ファン・オルデンボルフの芸術活動における重要な概念のひとつであるポリフォニー(多声音楽)の概念に対応するものだ。ポリフォニーには、多様な声だけでなく、声の交錯や同調、それぞれの境界線の内側で声が解き放たれ、集合的なリズムの形成が必要とされる。即興を政治活動の代替的な様式として肯定するためには、テリー・イーグルトンを参照するのがよい。イーグルトンは、政治の目的は「良い生活」を確保することだと主張する一方で、この「良い生活」はジャズの即興演奏をする音楽家たちの作業過程を通じて思い描くことができると論じている。

即興演奏をするジャズの楽団は、各メンバーが自分の好きなように自分を表現することが許されているという点において、交響楽団とは明らかに異なっている。しかし、ジャズの演奏家は、他のミュージシャンの自己表現的なパフォーマンスを受け入れる感性を持って即興演

訳注iv　インターセクショナリティ(またはインターセクショナリズム)とは、公民権を剥奪された異なるグループ、あるいはマイノリティのグループ間の「交差」の研究、特に、抑圧や差別の多層的なシステムの「交差」の研究である。

奏を行うのである。彼らが奏でる複雑なハーモニーは、共通の楽譜を演奏しているからではなく、一人ひとりの自由な音楽表現が、他のメンバーの自由な音楽表現の基礎となっている故に生まれる。一人ひとりが音楽的に雄弁になればなるほど、他のプレイヤーもそれに触発され、さらなる高みを目指そうとするのだ[6]。

ファン・オルデンボルフは、人々が進んで参加し、自分の考えや経験を提供してくれるという点で、自身が主催する集いにしばしば驚かされると述べている。そしてこの驚きの次に、彼女は「(私の作品の)参加者が、自分自身をどう認識し、作品のプロセスの中にどう位置付けているかはさまざまだと思うが、それは常に一種の交渉なのだ」[7]と付け加えている。研究の様式は即興的な実践の中にある。これこそ「民主主義」の基盤ではないだろうか? もっとも重要な全体というものは存在せず、各々が互いに調和している。

プンクトゥム[v]

《偽りなき響き》が撮影された、あるいは集会が行われた建物は、オランダと旧オランダ領東インド間の無線電信が初めて開始された一九二〇年頃に、放送局として建てられたラジオ・コートワイクである。初期モダニズム建築のこの建物は、ブルータリズムの壮大さと荒々しさを持ち、強い存在感を放っている。

6 Terry Eagleton, *The Meaning of Life* (Oxford University Press, 2007), 174. (テリー・イーグルトン『人生の意味とは何か』有泉学宙、高橋公雄、清水英之、松村美佐子訳、彩流社、二〇一三年。)

7 ウェンデリン・ファン・オルデンボルフ、KUNCI Cultural Studies Centerとの未発表のインタビュー、二〇〇八年。

訳註v ロラン・バルトによれば「ストゥディウム」は一般的、科学的関心を意味し、文化的にコード化された写真受容を指す。それに対して「プンクトゥム」は一般的な概念の体系を揺さぶり、それを破壊しにやってくるもので、コード化不可能な細部を発見してしまうような経験である。

訳註vi　社会的・歴史的に構築された規範がそれ自身を繰り返し引用しつつ不変の本質として実体化する作用を言う。

8　Rudolf Mrázek, Engineers of Happy Land: Technology and Nationalism in a Colony (Princeton, NJ: Princeton University Press, 2002).

しかし、「祖国」の声を植民地に届けるための機器（設置してすぐに時代遅れになったらしい）が全て撤去され、空っぽになった今では、そのそこはかとない空虚さが、決して語ることができないものの多くと共鳴している。この建物のバルコニーで「もし私がオランダ人であったなら」を読むエディーンのショットには、荒涼とした周囲の風景が垣間見える。映像が停止するたびに、言い換えれば、リハーサルの時の低い声や会話や笑い声によってパフォーマティビティ（行為遂行性）が中断されるたびに、建物のファサードが我々の眼前に立ち現れる。そしてこの場面では、風景から聞こえてくる音や鳥の鳴き声に続いて、オランダとインドネシアで親しまれ、どちらの国でもインドネシア語で歌われる子守唄が流れてくる。機能的には、子守唄は建物の内部で行われている集会への移行の瞬間を示しているが、言葉による交流に満ちたこの集いは、変化に富んだ静止や間、言葉から映像への逸脱によって遮られる。その様子は、ルドルフ・ムラウゼック[8]が言うところの、前世紀末のインドネシアにおけるラジオの仕組みを思い起こさせる。十九世紀後半の旧オランダ領東インドでの生活においては、電信、電話、郵便が多用され、ムラウゼックが示唆するように、異なる場所の間の近さ、近接性、接続性の感覚を醸し出していた。しかしムラウゼックは、ラジオという直接的な無線通信の登場によってこの多幸感は失われたと言及する。オランダ人は、第二次世界大戦で日本軍に降伏し植民地を失うことになる予感の中で、迫り来る憂鬱と郷愁を感じ、インドネシア人の間では植民地体制の差別的な支配からくる不満が高まっていた。ムラウゼックにとって当時のラジオは、何が起こるか誰にもわからない時代に、政治的・文化的な変化を知らせる一時的な装置であり、皮肉なことにそれは、絶え間なく続く会話や音楽のように聞こえるものとは全く違い、真空や沈黙を増幅するものだったのだ。

そしてここで、研究会やブリコラージュの状態とは言葉のやりとりだけでは定義できるものではないことが明らかになる。会話とその中で行われている交渉には、もうひとつ、語られることのない含みがある。私はそれを、ロラン・バルトの『明るい部屋』から「プンクトゥム」の概念を借りて名付けたいと思う。バルトは、写真の性質に関する記号論的というよりもむしろ反記号論的な説明において、プンクトゥムを、社会的、政治的、文化的規範によって定義される「ストゥディウム（ラテン語の「研究」から来た言葉）」という概念と対比させている。ストゥディウムに対抗するプンクトゥムとは、イメージの作者が意図することができない、ただ自然に現れるのを待つしかない偶発的な特徴や性質を指す。それは「時間」や「過ぎ去ったこと」[9]を体現する、チクっと刺された、あるいはつねられた時のような痛みを連想させるが、これは見る者と撮られる者との間の主観的な関係の経験として理解することができる。あるいは、これこそ「研究」を純粋に研究たらしめているものだとも言えるだろう。ハーニーとモートンの「研究」の概念は、「黒人」の概念によってのみ具体化することができ、彼らが研究と言う時、それは「ブラック・スタディ（黒人研究）」[vii]を意味している。集団的抵抗としての黒人研究は、農地の囲い込み、奴隷制、人種差別に対する黒人社会の痛々しくも粘り強い闘いの長い歴史の上に築かれてきた。我々は、苦痛に満ちているのに、はかなく、強く、人を自由にする彼らの闘いから学ぶと同時に、そこから学ぶことを意識的に手放そうとするのである。

9 「もはや形式ではなく、強度という範疇に属するこの新しいパンクトゥムとは、「時間」である。「写真」のノエマ《それは＝かつて＝あった》の悲痛な強調であり、その純粋な表象である」。ロラン・バルト『明るい部屋 写真についての覚書』花輪光訳、みすず書房、一九八五年、一一八頁。(Roland Barthes, *La Chambre claire: Note sur la photographie*, Paris: Gallimard, 1980.)

訳註vii 「ブラック・スタディ」とは、ディアスポラ全域のアフリカ人とアフリカ系住民の経験を研究し理解するための学際的・複合的アプローチである。

作品中に映し出される建物のファサードはプンクトゥムになっているが、あの進歩的な時代の建築家で
もこれを予期することは不可能だった。その意味は誰にも理解できないが、いつでもどこでも録音できる
鳥のさえずりは、音響的なプンクトゥムである。子守唄は誰にとってもプンクトゥムであるが、一人ひと
りの聞き手や歌い手は、自分だけの特別な記憶、かつては持っていたが今は失ってしまった記憶を持って
いる。そしてそれは、生まれ出ることによる母親からの別離と、その後、必然
的に死を共有するという体験にも似ている。[10]《偽りなき響き》に登場する集い、
あるいは我々が望む民主主義の形としての集いを作り出すある種の研究やブリ
コラージュは、プンクトゥムに出会い、それを容認することによって成立する
のだ。

今日の民主主義はプンクトゥムを知っているのだろうか。残念ながら、その制度的空間においてはプン
クトゥムは明らかに知られていない。世界中の広場は、連帯を求める叫びに涙しては、すぐにそれを拭い
去る人々で埋め尽くされているかもしれないが、議会の時空は、全ての音楽、全てのブリコラージュとプ
ンクトゥムを失った。《偽りなき響き》は、我々が自ら隠した涙の影で研究し即興することを忘れない限り、
他にどのような集いの時空がありうるかを思い出させてくれるのである。

二〇一五年十月執筆、二〇二二年十月改訂。

10　　　私的だが重要な注釈：この子
守唄を歌ったのは作家の娘である。ま
た、祖父母や母が住んでいたことから、
オランダ植民地時代のインドネシアと
作家には個人的な関係もある。

ビンナ・チョイ

ビンナ・チョイ

キュレーター。オランダのユトレヒトにあるCasco Art Institute: Working for the Commonsのディレクターとして、二元的な世界観やシステムに代わる、アートを通じた、あるいはアートのための「コモンズ」を探求している。主なプロジェクトに「Grand Domestic Revolution」(二〇〇九〜二〇二一年、田中麻衣子と協働)、「Site for Unlearning (Art Organization)」(二〇一四〜二〇一八年、アネット・クラウス、Cascoチームと協働)、「Travelling Farm Museum of Forgotten Skills」(二〇一八年から継続中、the Outsidersと協働)、「Electric Palm Tree」(崔敬華と協働)、「Unmapping Eurasia」(ミ・ユーと協働)などがある。第十一回光州ビエンナーレ「Eighth Climate (What does art do?)」のキュレーター、シンガポールビエンナーレ2022「Natasha」の共同芸術監督を務めた他、ドイツのケルンに拠点を置く「Academy of the Arts of the World」のメンバー、国際ネットワーク「AFIELD」のアドバイザーでもある。

《偽りなき響き》映像スチル

Film still from *No False Echoes*

〈ふたつの石〉映像スチル

Film still from *Two Stones*

《ヒア》撮影記録　撮影：ヤコプ・ダニレヴィッチ

Production still from *Hier*, photo by Jakub Danilewicz

《オブサダ》撮影記録 撮影：ヤコブ・ダニレヴィッチ

Production still from obsada, photo by Jakub Danilewicz

《ふたつの石》映像スチル

Film still from Two Stones

《ふたつの石》映像スチル

Film still from *Two Stones*

《彼女たちの》撮影記録

Production still from of girls

医学
490

〈偽りなき響き〉撮影記録　撮影：シルチオ・コルホフ

Production still from *No False Echoes*, photo by Sirtjo Koolhof

考察のイメージ

パブロ・デ・オカンポ

河野晴子　訳

映像作家のピーター・ワトキンスが一九六六年に発表した『ザ・ウォー・ゲーム』（The War Game）は、核攻撃を受けたイギリスのとある街の様子を描いた擬似ドキュメンタリー映画で、彼のもっとも有名な作品に挙げられるだろう。当初は BBC のために製作されたものだったが、そのあまりにショッキングな内容が一般のテレビ視聴者には不向きだという判断から放映は見送られた。ドキュメンタリーの形式と言語を用いて、ルポルタージュのニュース放送やインタビューを交えながら展開するワトキンスの映画は、異様なほどにリアリティの語調に近すぎたということである。物語としてもまた、『ザ・ウォー・ゲーム』は当時の状況や文脈と共鳴した。一九六〇年代と言えばまさに冷戦のピークであり、核戦争の脅威は現実味を帯びていた。おそらく事態がもっとも緊迫したのは、一九六〇年代初頭にキューバを舞台にソ連とアメリカが激しく対立した時であろう。

その後、二十年の歳月を経て、ワトキンスはこの映画の続きとして一九八七年に『旅程』（The Journey）を発表する。それほど多くの人に観られた映画ではなかったが、何年もかけて複数の国を舞台に製作され、上映時間が十四時間にも及ぶスケールの大きさもあり、なかなか仰々しい映画として受け止められたのは確かである。『ザ・ウォー・ゲーム』と同様、『旅程』は冷戦と、第二次世界大戦の終末から一九八〇年代まで続く核兵器の拡散に深く関わる映画である。しかしながら、その社会政治的文脈と、軍産複合体批判と核廃絶への取り組みという大まかな目的を同じくしつつも、この二つの映画はそれぞれ異なる戦略とアプローチを示している。

一言で言えば、ドキュメンタリーやノンフィクション映画は観る者に対して真実の一端を伝えたり、示

唆することを目指すものだ。たとえば『ザ・ウォー・ゲーム』は、核戦争の脅威のより包括的な理解を広め、原爆による爆風を思弁的なイメージとして描き、核武装の危険性に警鐘を鳴らすことを使命としている。『旅程』も同様の反核メッセージを掲げるという目的にかなうものであったが、こちらは完成した作品であると同時にプロセスを中心に構築された映画であった。

『旅程』は人々が共に学び、交流する中で進行する製作プロセスがしっかりと擦り合ってできたひとつの成果物だったと言える。映し出される個々人はいずれも登場人物や被写体ではなく、映画の製作者たちと対話をする能動的な役割を担っている。撮影は十五カ国をまたぎ、参加者たちはそれぞれの専門知識や見解を持ち寄っているが、特権的な立場から発言しているわけではない。参加者たちは核軍備競争の影響に直接的・間接的にさらされた自身の体験を語り合い、互いに、そして製作者に質問を投げかけている。ワトキンスの『旅程』は観客に情報を伝えることを単なる最終目的としていたのではなく、製作に携わる全ての関係者の間に協働的な学びの交流を喚起する作品であったのだ。

私は『旅程』に見られるこの協働製作の形式を念頭に、同様の性質を持つウェンデリン・ファン・オルデンボルフの映像作品に考えを巡らせている。ワトキンスと同様、彼女の作品も「リアルであるもの」を投影し表象するドキュメンタリー映画の手法をとっているが、最終的にはより繊細な表現となっている。ファン・オルデンボルフの映像作品の独特な強みは主題をめぐる考察をイメージとして作り出している点にある。これらの作品で彼女は、考察のイメージを作ることは切り取りや構図ではなく、むしろプロセスの問題であることを明らかにしている。つまりイメージとは何かではなく、どのようにしてイメージを作

るか、ということである。

「ウェンデリン・ファン・オルデンボルフ　柔らかな舞台」に展示されるもっとも初期の映像作品《マウリッツ・スクリプト》（二〇〇六年）は、短めのカットを繋ぐ形で登場人物たちを紹介している。オランダ・ハーグのマウリッツハイス美術館（旧オランダ領ブラジル総督を務めたヨハン・マウリッツ・ファン・ナッサウの旧居でもある）の金装飾が施された壁の前で近距離から撮影された男女たちは、十七世紀中頃のオランダ領ブラジルで活躍した重要な人物たちの役柄を担っている。冒頭のクレジットタイトルが流れるにつれ、人物はそれぞれ複数の参加者によって表されていることがわかる。

参加者のひとりが机の上に置かれた一冊の本を読み始める。一見すると美術館の室内を思わせるような、権力と歴史の重みを感じさせる美しく綴じられた本である。しかしページがめくられると、厚い書物のところどころに文字が印刷されたA4の紙が挟み込まれているのが見える。本来の重厚な書物は注釈が施され、複雑なものとなり、手が加えられているのだ。女性が声に出して読み上げる物語の断片から、ヨハン・マウリッツ・ファン・ナッサウが旧オランダ領ブラジルで総督を務めた間に経験した出来事の数々が年代記として立ち上がる。

場面が展開するにつれ、さまざまな参加者が登場し、複数の視点からこの歴史をめぐる発言をする。スクリーン上の人物たちは芝居をしているわけでも朗読をしているわけでもない。彼・彼女らは能動的に声に出して文章を読み上げている。些細な違いに思えるが、この振る舞いこそが考察のイメージを作り上げ

71　　　　パブロ・デ・オカンポ

るのに欠くことができないのだ。さらに特筆すべきは、全ての参加者が美術館という公共の場所にいることである。考察のセッションは大抵ひとりの人物を近距離から捉える構図で進められるが、時折その後ろを撮影クルーや美術館の来館者が通り過ぎていくのが見える。こうした映像は重要な特徴を示している——これは声を出して行っている公の考察なのだ。オランダによるブラジルの植民地統治は期間こそ短かったものの、読み上げられる文章からこの時代の残酷な影響が決して小さくはなかったことがわかる。それぞれ異なるバックグラウンドを持つ参加者たちは、何百年も昔の出来事を詳細に掘り下げ、この歴史が現代のオランダ社会に与え続けている影響を鑑みながら、かつての出来事との結びつきを見出そうとしているのだ。

《マウリッツ・スクリプト》には、ファン・オルデンボルフの映像作品を構成する多くの要素が見られる。建築物、文章、そして参加者のグループ。彼女の映像作品に特有なこれらの要素は、いずれの場合も互いに有機的な繋がりを持つよう組み合わされて機能している。つまり、彼女の映像作品は本についてでも、建物についてでも、個人についてでもないということだ。こうした要素が組み合わさってひとつの映像を構成し、質問を投げかけ、参加者同士で考察を共有する、その経験を生み出すのである。

これらの映像は文章的だと言えるだろう。いわゆる演劇やドラマの形式に倣うような、演者のために脚色された「物語」を台本とし、そこから派生するということではない。文章はファン・オルデンボルフの作品の土台となる問いかけを始める点、すなわち教育モデルを提供しているのだ。ここに用いられる文章は真実を声高に主張したり、実証するためのものではない。正史の欄外にあるものと関わることを促し、

時間や文化理解の境界を超えて個人的な繋がりや共鳴を拾い上げるために用いられているのだ。

ファン・オルデンボルフの映像作品の多くには登場人物や被写体がいるが、大抵それはスクリーン上に映し出される実際の人たちではない。映像の中で言及され、時にその言葉が引用される歴史上の人物たちである。いずれの人物も単に与えられた台詞を読み上げるのではなく、積極的に映像に関わるコラボレーターの役割を担っていることからも、参加者と呼ぶべき存在だろう。参加者は自分の物語を語るだけでなく、問いかけのプロセスに関わるためにその人自身として映像に現れる。文章を読み、他の参加者と会話をし、自分が住む場所とその歴史を問うコラボレーターたちは現代的な主題としてカメラに収められている。

こうした参加者が単なる登場人物ではないのと同様、彼・彼女らがいる場所もまた単なるセットや背景ではない。そこに映る建築物は人物と同じで、あらゆる共鳴と関係性に満ちている。ファン・オルデンボルフはそのプロセスを通して、建築物がどのようにして歴史を反映するかを探求する。建築物の空間を舞台に、それらを設計し、建設した人々、数々の歴史的機能、そして現在そこに住まう人々との間に対話を生み出しているのだ。《マウリッツ・スクリプト》はその歴史的主題にとって重要であるマウリッツハイス美術館で撮影されたものだが、《偽りなき響き》(二〇〇八年)という別の初期作品は旧オランダ領東インド(現在のインドネシア)に向けて初めてラジオ放送を行った放送局跡地、ラジオ・コートワイクを舞台としている。

《ふたつの石》（二〇一九年）と題された作品は、初期の《マウリッツ・スクリプト》のように一冊の本の描写から始まる。冒頭の場面は集合住宅地の中庭である。ミディアムショットで捉えられたベンチに座る女性が膝の上に置いた本から一文を読み上げる。「どの文書を開いても今さら驚くこともないことに改めて気づかされる。言わずもがなだが、過ぎし日々の言葉はその時代に固定されることはなく、むしろ無造作に現在に吐き戻される」。この一文が、二人の人物、二つの場所の間、そして「過ぎし日々」から「現在」までの複数の一時性を横断してひとつの物語を構成している。

映像は、共に一九三〇年代にソ連で活動し、戦後オランダに暮らした建築家のロッテ・スタム＝ベーゼと、カリブ海出身の活動家で著述家のヘルミナ・ハウスヴァウトの二人の女性の軌跡を繋いでいる。参加者たちの語りを通して、彼女たちと撮影場所の詳細が見えてくる。ひとつは一九三〇年代にウクライナのハルキウ、もうひとつは一九五〇年代オランダのロッテルダムに建てられたものである。スタム＝ベーゼはこの両方の建築を手がけている。ひとつは一九三〇年代にウクライナのハルキウ、もうひとつは一九五〇年代オランダのロッテルダムに建てられたものである。スタム＝ベーゼはバウハウスで建築を学んだ最初の女性のうちのひとりで、複数のコミュニティの共存を目指したある種ユートピア的ビジョンの体現としてこれらの集合住宅を設計した。映像に参加するのは全て女性で、彼女たちはこの集合住宅地の優れた点や影響について語られる一方、それに対抗する形でハウスヴァウトが一九七〇年代に示した視点が導入される。ハウスヴァウトはロッテルダムの各地区でカリブ海出身のオランダ人の割合を制限したかつての住宅政策を批判し、こうした政策がスタム＝ベーゼが思い描いた理想的なコミュニティに悪影響を及ぼしたと主張している。

こうした複数の物語や視点が、ファン・オルデンボルフの映像の形式の中に集約されている。《ふたつの石》はシングルチャンネルの映像作品であるが、三十分ほど経ったところで映像のリピート再生が始まる。コマは前半と同じ順番で進むが、二巡目には異なる音声編集のサウンドトラックが添えられている。繰り返して見てみると、意図的な音の編集が明確に浮かび上がってくる。映像には多くの人が登場し、終始彼女たちの声が聞こえてくるが、実際には音とイメージは同期されていない。映像には多くの人が登場し、終始彼女ン・オルデンボルフは映像に全く新しい会話を織り込むことができるのだ。この非同期性があることで、ファン・オルデンボルフは映像に全く新しい会話を織り込むことができるのだ。この非同期性があることで、ファの、登場人物たちはその都度異なる感情を表現している。こうした映像の構造こそが物語の中の会話や言及を押し広げ、各部分が円を描いて元に戻るように参加者たちは時間の経過の中で自分自身と対話をするのだ。

たとえばあるシーンの一巡目の音声トラックでは、参加者のハンナ・ドーン・ヘンダーソンが変化と進化というものの限界についてこう述べている。「台所をなくしたからといって女性に対する抑圧の歴史が消えはしない」。この同じシーンが繰り返される二巡目では、彼女自身が人種差別を受けた過去について、そして最終的には希望をもって多少なりともこの無力さを乗り越えることができたと語っている。

《ヒア》(二〇一一年)は、アーネム美術館のアーチ型天井の部屋の映像から始まる。そこにはギター、ベース、ウクレレを弾く若い女性たちのバンド、FREDがいる。彼女たちが奏でるのはインドネシアの大衆音楽の一種であるクロンチョン。その控えめなメロディが部屋を満たすと、今度は他二名の参加者の声が

聞こえてくる。そのうちのひとりがクロンチョンのインド・ヨーロッパ的な音楽性について語り、ある時点でこれを「メランコリックな植民地の歌」と呼んでいる。バンドが演奏を続ける中、参加者のララ・ヌーベルグとペルミ・アデジュモは美術館のさまざまな部屋を歩いて回る。時折、バンドによる曲の演奏も挿入される。彼女たちはクロンチョンをヨーロッパの植民地政策の産物と位置付け、オランダに住むインド・ヨーロッパ人たちにとっての文化的関連性やノスタルジックな性質について語りながら、その歴史の概要を浮き彫りにする。

ヌーベルグとアデジュモは共に文筆家であるが、映像の中のテキスト、つまり会話と問いかけの展開にとって基礎となる要素は音楽である。彼女たちにとってそれは内省や反応を誘発するものなのだ。インド・ヨーロッパ系であるヌーベルグは、奏でられる曲を自身の母親と祖母、そしてオランダに来る以前に遡る自身の家系と関連付けている。彼女は旧オランダ領東インドというかつての植民地出身でありながら、近代インドネシアとは繋がりのない自分の家族の言わば中間的な存在性について語る。一方のアデジュモはナイジェリア出身の詩人であるが、ビリー・アイリッシュやフレディ・マーキュリーといった別の音楽的関心から個人的な回想を語り始める。クロンチョンの調べに耳を傾けると、故郷や記憶に関する静かな思いが彼女の中で呼び起こされる。広間を満たす音に包まれながら彼女はこんな言葉を紡ぐ――「聴いたことがない音楽の夢は見られる？ それはきっと帰り道を見失った生まれ故郷のよう」。

映像の中で奏でられる音楽の伝統と同様、いずれの女性も自身の異種混交的なルーツ、ディアスポラ、アイデンティティ、そして文化的帰属という観点から発言をしている。ここでは彼女たちの人生に思いを

めぐらせるひとつの枠組みとして音楽が用いられているが、建物もまた観る者に対して別の枠組みを開いている。十九世紀に建てられたアーネム美術館は、元々は社会的地位の低い男性、つまり「植民地出身」の男性たちの社交場として使われていた。映像の中の美術館は大規模な改修の最中で、壁は骨組みが剥き出しになるまでに解体され、足場が組まれている。粗くくり抜かれたコンクリートはかつてドアがあった場所だ。こうした変容のプロセスのただ中にある建物は、植民地時代の過去が何か別のものに変わりつつあることを示している。

こうした全ての瞬間がバンドの演奏する曲の断片によって強調される。ある場面では、七十八回転のレコードに針を落とす手元をカメラが上から捉えている。聞こえてくるスクラッチノイズは伝統的なクロンチョンの一節である。しばらくレコードの調べに合わせた後、ＦＲＥＤの面々は自分たちの曲へと演奏を切り替える。彼女たちがようやく途切れることなく曲を奏でるのは、映像のラスト数分のところである。ここまで彼女たちは、クロンチョンという音楽の形式に聴き入り、練習をし、理解を深めている。映像の背景で流れていた彼女たちの演奏が、この音楽的系譜の要素を内包しながらここで初めてオリジナルの曲に再編成されているのだ。

《オブサダ》(二〇二一年) と題された作品は、一定のリズムの荒い息遣いで始まる。カメラは板張りの床の上に置かれた椅子を俯瞰で捉えている。画面外から二人の人物の声が聞こえてくる。

「集中してる」

「私も」

この言葉には軽く二重の意味が込められている。初めは参加者のひとりの計算された息遣いについてであるが、場面が展開するにつれ、映像に映らない二人目がカメラのピントを合わせている動作について言及していることがわかる。映像の舞台はポーランドにあるウッチ美術館とウッチ映画大学の二カ所である。カメラがフレームインしたり、ブームマイクが見えるなど、制作の様子を見せることはこれまでのファン・オルデンボルフの作品に共通することだが、ここでは制作のプロセスと撮影クルーそのものが映像の主題となっている。二つの建物に集う女性たちはカメラの前で対話をしたり、ファン・オルデンボルフと共に映像制作に携わるクルーとして作品に参加している。女性たちは大学での勉強、両親や家族、あるいはこれまでのキャリア上の選択や映像制作の中で担ってきた種々の役割を互いに比べ合うなど、この作品への参加に至るまでのさまざまな経験について自由に語り合う。会話の中で繰り返し語られるのは、ジェンダーバイアスの影響について。彼女たちは、女性だからといいように利用されたり、領域を侵されたり、高圧的な男性の同僚に怒鳴られたり、仕事をしていく上でこのような差別や偏見に絶えず我慢しなければならないことなどについて語り続ける。

彼女たちの会話は、一連の振り付けされたポーズやカメラレンズの前に透明な色付きのアクリル板を掲げる実験的なフレーミングによっていくつかに分割されている。こうした要素は、ウッチ映画大学に端を発する特定の歴史的出来事を参照するものである。それは「ワークショップ・オブ・ザ・フィルム・フォ

ルム」という、映画の形式と構造を根本から考え直す学生によるムーブメントで、そこでは映像の形式に関わるさまざまな実験に加え、革新的な制作プロセスそのものにも盲点はあった。参加者には女性が含まれていたものの、このワークショップを推し進めた理念そのものを目指すべく協働的な制作が行われていた。しかし、ワークショップは極めて男性優位の場であり、多くの前衛芸術の潮流がそうであったように、大部分の女性は除外され、忘れ去られた存在であった。

映像の中の女性たちはワークショップの歴史を記録した写真に見入り、当時のプロジェクトを自分たちなりに再現してみせる。そのうちのひとつ、一九七三年にウッチ美術館で開かれた実験を彷彿とさせるのは、カメラが透明な膜を通して反射や映像イメージを捉える箇所である。映像は二つに分かれたり、重ねられたり、あるいは覆われて見えなくなる。こうした一九七〇年代のワークショップには確かに女性が含まれていたが、一九七一年の映画『開かれたかたち——女優の顔の上での遊び』(Open Form—Game on an Actress' Face)に見られるように、女性は映像作家が実験を行うためのただの面としても扱われることもあった。ファン・オルデンボルフの作品の女性たちは今まさにこの歴史を再考し、集合的にその中に自分たちを介入させているのだ。

これに先立つ場面では、女性たちがドイツの映像作家、ヘルケ・ザンダーの一九七八年の映画『全面的に矮小化された人格——ReduPers』(The All-Around Reduced Personality—ReduPers)の映像を見ている。これはシングルマザーで写真家の女性(ザンダー自身が演じている)が家計をやりくりすることに苦労している様子を伝える作品である。ベルリンで仕事をしていたザンダーだが、彼女はウッチでのワークショッ

プと同時代に活躍しており、ファン・オルデンボルフがここで彼女を取り上げるのは、この時代に女性がさまざまな形で映像の形式を試みていた事例に光を当てるためだと言える。もちろん、こうした表現は観客のためだけではない。《オブサダ》の参加者もまた作品のプロセスの中で学んでいるのだ。特筆すべきは、ファン・オルデンボルフによる『全面的に矮小化された人格——ReduPers』の引用が、この映画自体と呼応している点である。ザンダーもまた自身の作品の中でイヴォンヌ・レイナーやヴァリー・エクスポートといった女性の映像作家が手がけた作品を引用しているからである。

ファン・オルデンボルフのこれまでの作品は必ずと言っていいほど女性の参加者に焦点が当てられてきたが、これら三つの近作では共通して女性の参加が直接的にジェンダーの主題に関わっている。《ふたつの石》の冒頭では、ヘルミナ・ハウスヴァウトが機関誌『黒人労働者』(*The Negro Worker*)に書き綴った階級闘争、人種差別、性差別が交わる点、すなわち彼女が思う有色人種の労働者階級の女性であることの意味が参照される。この主張がひとつの枠組みとなり、映像の参加者たちはハウスヴァウトとスタム゠ベーゼのフェミニスト的思想から派生するさまざまな意見に対する自分の立ち位置を考えることができるのである。《ヒ

ア》では、参加者たちが改装中の美術館の広間に集まっている。女性たちの存在そのものが、権力、歴史的遺産、表象を体現するこの建物の構造を積極的に再定義していることが確かに感じられる。そして《オブサダ》に登場する女性たちは、共に経験した映画産業における性差別について回顧し、彼女たちが期待する変化が果たしてこの業界で実現可能なのかという議論で話を終える。

訳註 i　黒人労働組合国際委員会が一九二八年から一九三七年まで発刊していた機関誌。

「古い世代と新しい世代の架け橋である私たちはもう負けている？　それとも勝負はまだ……」

「負けてないと思うけど。甘いかな」

「私たちがいなくならないと変わらない？」

映像の中の彼女たちの会話に結論や答えはない。ファン・オルデンボルフの映像作品を通した考察は決定的な何かをもたらすことはない。彼女と考察を共にする参加者たちは、絶えず生成するプロセスのただ中で自分が果たす役割を模索している。「変化は誰かが起こすもの。それは私たちかもしれない」と。

パブロ・デ・オカンポ

パブロ・デ・オカンポ

ミネソタ州ミネアポリスにあるウォーカー・アート・センターの
ディレクター兼ムービング・イメージのキュレーター。二〇一四年
から二〇二〇年までカナダ・バンクーバーのアーティスト・ラン・
センター、Western Frontにて展覧会キュレーターを務めた他、
二〇〇六年から二〇一四年までトロントのイメージズ・フェスティ
バルの芸術監督、オレゴン州ポートランドで開催されるシネマ・プ
ロジェクトの共同設立者兼コレクティブ・メンバー、二〇一三年に
は第五十九回 Robert Flaherty Film Seminar「History is What's
Happening」のプログラマーなどを歴任。
『Canadian Art』『C Magazine』『BlackFlash』などの雑誌や
『Dissident Lines: Lis Rhodes』(Nottingham Contemporary,
二〇一九年)、『Low Relief: Lucy Raven (EMPAC, Mousse,
Portikus, 二〇一八年)などのカタログに寄稿。

《偽りなき響き》映像スチル

Film still from *No False Echoes*

《オブサダ》映像スチル

Film still from *obsada*

《ふたつの石》映像スチル

Film still from *Two Stones*

〈オブサダ〉映像スチル

Film still from obsada

《ふたつの石》映像スチル

Film still from *Two Stones*

《ヒア》映像スチル

Film still from *Hier*.

〈マウリッツ・スクリプト〉映像スチル

Film still from *Maurits Script*

ウェンデリン・ファン・オルデンボルフ：インタビュー

アンドリュー・マークル

東京、二〇二二年九月十四日

良知暁　訳

91

アンドリュー・マークル（AM）：これまでの制作活動について改めて調べながら、自分があなたの作品に繰り返し現れる三角関係を辿っているような地理的な感覚を覚えました。たとえば、オランダ、インドネシア、ブラジルあるいは中南米という地理的な繋がりがあります。この関係はオランダ植民地主義の輪郭をゆるやかに描き出していますね。他にも、映画と建築と音楽の交わりがあります。なぜ、このようなテーマに関心を持ち続けているのでしょうか。

ウェンデリン・ファン・オルデンボルフ（WvO）：地理的な繋がりについては私自身の生い立ちも関係しています。母が生まれた場所ということもあり、インドネシアに対する関心は家族史的なものから生まれました。オランダ人は三百年にわたってインドネシアを統治していましたが、一九四九年の植民地解放を機に、インドネシア系オランダ人やオランダ人約三十万人が本国に引き揚げました。彼らがオランダにもたらした影響は、食文化から一九五〇年代に大流行した音楽ジャンル「インドロック」に至るありとあらゆるところに表れています。ブラジルは、私がこの二十年間に家族とたくさんの時間を過ごした土地で、家族との思い出を通じた個人的な繋がりもありますが、ある時、そう言えばブラジルもオランダの植民地だったことに気づきました。

言うまでもないことですが、作品が生い立ちのみに還元されてしまうことは望んでいません。しかし、個人的な体験を起点にした深い理解に基づいて制作する時、アーティストはとても優れた作品を生み出すものです。生きることを通じて培った感情的な理解だけでなく、そこに知的なものを加えることができます。もちろん、私が制作する全ての作品がオランダ植民地主義の遺産を扱うわけではありません。ただこうした問題に取り組み始めた二〇〇五、二〇〇六年頃、当時はオランダ植民地主義や、それが住宅問題や家父長制といった現代のオランダ社会の問題とどのように結びついているのかについて関心を寄せるアー

ティストはほとんどいなかったと思います。そして、《偽りなき響き》（二〇〇八年）は、そうしたリサーチから生まれました。

AM：映画、建築、音楽の関係性についてはどうでしょうか。

WvO：映画に対しては、それが情動をさまざまな重なりや形で示すことのできる多面的なメディウムであるとして、昔から憧れを抱いてきました。けれどもいざ扱ってみると、最初の頃は全く取り付く島もありませんでした。ある時、映画制作の方法を何か他のものを作るために利用できないかと思いつき、実験的なアプローチを試みることにしました。映画制作を装いながら制作するとはどういうことなのか、と。
いろいろと試してみて、映像作品として最初に制作したのが《マウリッツ・スクリプト》（二〇〇六年）です。この作品では脚本だけを用意して、それ以降は映画制作の手順を概念的にのみ辿っていきました。鑑賞者が自分の意見や知識だけでなく、他人の意見や知識を取り入れながら作る方法を探っていたのです。そこで私は自分が本当に編集があらゆる声や考え方を読み取れるように編集について学ぶ必要があり、そこで私は自分が本当に編集が好きだと気づきました。私は時々DJをするのですが、編集は構築的かつ律動的であるという点で音楽とも深い関連性があります。メタ的な位置に立ち、構築的に思考し、そしてリズムに身を任せる。そうでなければうまくいきません。

AM：そのような考えは音楽の使い方にも影響しています。

WvO：音楽は作品に異なる洞察力をもたらします。それは言説でもイメージでもなく、音楽特有の情動と感情と情報が組み合わさったものです。ただ、作品で音楽を使うのは、撮影に参加する人が音楽特有の情動と感情と情報が組み合わさったものです。ただ、作品で音楽を使うのは、撮影に参加する人が音楽特有の情動と感情と音楽を使うのは、撮影に参加する人が音楽特有の情動と歌っ

たりする必要がある場合のみです。サウンドトラックとして音楽を使ったことは一度もありません。

AM：ということは、《偽りなき響き》や《ヒア》（二〇二一年）において、クロンチョンという音楽ジャンルを取り入れたのは、それが現代のオランダ社会の複雑なリアリティを伝えるための方法になると思ったからということですね。

WvO：はい。クロンチョンは十六世紀にインドネシアとポルトガルが接触したことから生まれた音楽です。弦楽器を組み込んだ近代音楽の一種で、十九世紀にインドネシア系オランダ人の劇団がこの列島で共通語として使われていたマレー語の歌詞を付けたことで普及していきました。地元の人々とオランダ系植民者の間で板挟みになっていた人々が、自分たちの声で自分たちを表現することができたという点で、クロンチョンは解放の音楽でした。決してハイカルチャーとして受け入れられることはありませんでしたが、グラモフォンの導入やレコード会社の国際的な大衆文化市場の拡張戦略もあって、驚異的な流行を見せました。ただ、クロンチョンには元々メランコリックな響きがあり、植民地解放と引き揚げの時代を経て、それはオランダ人が植民時代を懐かしむノスタルジックな音楽になりました。

《偽りなき響き》では、オランダの植民政策、旧オランダ東インド会社によるラジオ放送の統制について扱いました。映像の中で当時八歳の私の娘が「ニナ・ボボ」（"Nina Bobo"）を歌っていますが、驚いたことに娘はオランダの学校ですでにこの歌を習っていました。《ヒア》では、それぞれインドネシア、スリナム、オランダを含む幅広いバックグラウンドを持つ女性だけのバンド「FRED」のメンバーに、クロンチョンを分析し、現代的な視点から再制作してもらうように頼みました。それからもうひとりの主要人物、インドネシア系オランダ人のバックグラウンドを持つララに、四代遡るとインドネシアに辿り着く

彼女の家族史とクロンチョンとの繋がりについて話してもらいました。《ヒア》（hier：オランダ語で「ここ」の意味）というタイトルが示している通り、私は現代の若者が同時代性や行為主体性をどのように表現するのかに焦点を当てようと思っていましたが、むしろセンチメンタルな作品になったのかもしれません。音楽や映画は巧みに感情を揺さぶります。

AM：《ふたつの石》（二〇一九年）では全く異なる方法論が採用されていますね。同作では、一九三〇年代のソビエト連邦時代のウクライナのハルキウ・トラクター工場（KhTZ）の集合住宅と、一九五〇年代に建設されたオランダのロッテルダムにあるペンドレヒトという二つの大規模な住宅計画を扱うと共に、ドイツ人建築家のロッテ・スタム＝ベーゼとカリブ人アクティビストのヘルミナ・ハウスヴァウトという二人の実在の人物を中心に据えています。そして、視覚的なものと聴覚的なものと字幕を互いに衝突させることで、鑑賞者の注意をさまざまな方向に導いています。ここにはブレヒトの異化効果が働いていますね。

WvO：《ふたつの石》では、鑑賞者がロッテ・スタム＝ベーゼとヘルミナ・ハウスヴァウトの両者に、噛み合う部分と噛み合わない部分があると同時に感じることが大事だと考えていました。ロッテもヘルミナも平等の精神を掲げるが故に社会主義思想のイデオロギーに傾倒していました。しかし、ロッテが誰にとっても平等な建築を作ることに専念し、その平等が白人に限られたものであったのに対し、ヘルミナは住宅への平等なアクセスからスリナム系オランダ人住民を排除していた一九七〇年代のロッテルダムの住宅法に対する反対運動に取り組みました。平等という価値観を共有していたにもかかわらず、両者の間には相容れないものがありました。それはちょうどインターセクショナリティをめぐる今日的な議論に見られる

　　　　　　　　　　　　ウェンデリン・ファン・オルデンボルフ：

ように、白人フェミニズムと欧米の人種差別に対する闘争との関係が常に協力的だったわけではないということです。

この作品では、こうした世に知られていない歴史を掘い上げようとしました。実際、私はペンドレヒトに関心を持ち、この戦後の重要な都市計画になぜ女性が携わることができたのかを知りたいと思うまでは、バウハウスで最初の女性建築家になったロッテのこともほとんど知りませんでした。ロッテを突き動かしていたのは平等な住宅というビジョンでしたが、いまやペンドレヒトは当初の意図を完全に無視する形で、全てのユニットが民営化されて市場で取引される物件になってしまいました。こうした歴史を単に過ぎ去ったものと考えることはできません。また、資本主義や家父長制に触れることなく植民地主義を語ることなどできません。それらは全て繋がっています。

AM：ジェンダーやフェミニズムの問題を扱った近作《オブサダ》(obsada：ポーランド語で「キャスト」の意味）（二〇二一年）では、キャストも撮影クルーも全て女性でしたね。

WVO：まず話しておきたいのは、私の作品は探究の対象であり目的であるということです。自ら設定した問いに対する答えをあらかじめ用意することはありません。《オブサダ》の場合は、若い女性たちが未だに男性優位が続く映画産業の中で、自分たちの未来をどのように思い描くのかを知りたいと思いました。たとえば、私はいつも新しいプロジェクトに取り掛かるにあたって、女性の撮影クルーを探すのですがなかなか見つかりません。あちこちにいるにもかかわらず、すぐには見つからないのです。この時はポーランド最大の映画学校、ウッチ映画大学の学生や卒業生と一緒に制作しました。撮影が始まる直前に、ある学生が権力の乱用について発言したことをきっかけに、大学では激しい議論が交わされていました。あら

かじめ作品で扱おうと考えていたわけではなかったけれど、この議題は撮影内の対話でも言及されました。この映画大学に入らなかったからそうした教育に苦しめられずに済んで良かったと発言するキャストがいたり。こうした問題を話し合う機会がなかったので、彼女たちが語り始めたのには驚きました。特に、彼女たちが女性として映画産業で直面する困難や不安について語る機会はなかったので。それは期待以上のものになりました。

AM：あたかも作品内のパフォーマティブな要素が厄祓いとして機能しているかのようですね。

長い歴史のある空間でキャストが話したり、何らかの行為をすることで、鑑賞者にとってその空間の歴史が表面化し、結果としてその考古学的な行為が厄祓いの役目を果たす。《オブサダ》では空間それ自体が折り重ねられているように見えるからなのか、そのことをより一層強く感じました。

WvO：ウッチ映画大学内のセットで撮影したのですが、クシシュトフ・キェシロフスキも学生時代のロマン・ポランスキーも撮影しています。その空間は練習用に建てられたものなので、学生はセットを組んだり壁を塗ったり自由に使うことができました。ただ私がもっとも惹かれたのは、高いところに上がってセットを見下ろせるところで、おそらくそれ故に空間が折り重なっているように見えたのではないでしょうか。

《オブサダ》のもうひとつのロケ地は美術館で、これもまたウッチにあり、そこでは一九七〇年代に男性のみで構成された前衛集団「ワークショップ・オブ・ザ・フィルム・フォルム」が歴史的なパフォーマンスを繰り広げ、その表現を発展させていきました。撮影した中には、普段は構成主義の先駆的アーティスト、カタジナ・コブロの作品が展示されている部屋もありました。彼女は一九二〇年代にいかなる向き

も前後も上下もないラディカルな彫刻を提唱しています。ガラスの台座に据えられた彼女の作品にインスピレーションを得て、撮影の中で自分たちの身体を用いて造形するという実験に取り組みました。私が撮影監督に「特定のカメラポジションがなかったら、どのように撮影するだろうか」と尋ね、そのことについて話し合った結果、彼女はしゃがみこんでガラス越しに見上げるなど、とても自由に撮影しました。

AM：次に新作となる《彼女たちの》（二〇二二年）についてお聞きします。本作のロケ地のひとつは小説家の林芙美子が生前暮らした邸宅ですね。映画における日本家屋の歴史には長いものがありますが、そうした場所で撮影することについてどう考えていますか。

WvO：そのことについて、撮影監督の飯岡幸子さんがローポジションで撮影するかどうか聞いてくれたのですが、そうしていいものかどうか悩みました。小津安二郎がやったこととして誰もが知っていますから。ただ、戸外から撮影することにしたので、ローポジションから撮る以外にないと判断しました。日本家屋は、はっきりとした規格構造を持ち開放的な造りなので、どの方向を見通すこともできるような気になります。というわけで、屋外のカメラから屋内の人物に寄ったり、その動きを追ったりすることにしました。

芙美子が自邸を自ら設計したことは興味深いです。それはまるで小説家としての彼女が自邸を物語として書き上げたようなもので、私はその家を読み、制作を通して彼女の表現を分析したいと考えています。

AM：その他のロケ地にはどのように取り組みましたか。

WvO：主なロケ地である「元映画館」では、宮本百合子とその同棲相手の湯浅芳子に焦点を当てる予定です。

建築そのものというよりも一九五〇年代に開館した小さな映画館という機能に関心があり、それは芙美子の作品を原作とした成瀬巳喜男の映画を連想させるところもあります。近年、若手建築家たちが改修を手がけたことで、現在はレトロなインテリアを設えた雰囲気の良いバーのような場所になっています。現代の東京で快適に過ごすにはとても良い場所で、映画撮影という観点から見た時にも空間的に興味深い要素がたくさんあります。

また、前川國男が一九五〇年代初頭に手がけた初期の公共建築のひとつ、神奈川県立図書館でも短いシーンを撮影します。芙美子が日中戦争やアジア太平洋戦争期に日本の植民地や占領地域で執筆したものについて話し合うために、書物やアーカイブなどが収められた場所を探していました。前川のこの戦後モダニズム建築は、芙美子のこの時期の作品が前面に押し出す複雑な権力関係を反映しています。

AM：本作の主要人物である林芙美子と宮本百合子についてもう少し詳しく教えてもらいたいのですが、二人のどのようなところに興味を持ったのでしょうか。

WvO：建築や音楽や映画についてはすでに触れましたが、ここでは二十世紀初頭に女性やフェミニストが主に採用した表現方法である文学を扱っています。文学は彼女たちが自らを表現する第一の手段でした。芙美子と百合子は同時代を生きていながら、とても対照的だったので、私は二人の対話の場を作ろうと思いました。芙美子は極貧家庭の出身から大成した小説家にまで成り上がりましたが、百合子は裕福な家庭に育ち高等教育を受け、そこから貧しい人々への連帯を示しました。どちらも階級問題に共感していましたが、その表し方には大きな違いがあります。

芙美子の文体はとても情熱的で生々しくて、そこに心から惹かれます。彼女はあけすけでありながら美

しい文体で自らの女性性やセクシュアリティを物語ります。そこに私の好きなパンク的な側面があります。

一方、百合子は自らの政治性にとても自覚的です。彼女はジャン゠リュック・ゴダールがそうであったように政治性をめぐる物語を書き上げるのですが、それがまた教条的でもある。ある女性と七年にわたり同棲したことのある百合子は、社会主義的なイデオロギーへの忠誠のために自らのクィアの歴史を否定しているようでした。私はずっと社会主義と同性愛に対する寛大さには関係があると考えてきたので、そのことがとても複雑かつ奇妙なことに感じました。

芙美子と百合子の全貌は掴めなくとも、彼女たちの態度には現代の政治やこの時代に若者がどう応答すべきかが映し出されていると思います。参加者が朗読するテキストを探すにあたり、自分の初期の作品でも参加者に朗読してもらったことを思い出しました。本作でもこの二人の女性の作品や生涯を研究している若者がいます。歴史上実在した声が現在の若者を通じて共鳴することに期待を寄せています。

AM：まさに、トランプ主義からプーチンによるウクライナへの侵攻、そして、世界中で高まる環境危機など、数十年前、現役の若い世代が生まれたばかりの頃には考えられなかったような地球規模の紛争がすぐ側まで迫っていると感じますね。

百合子は一九四九年に「ファシズムは生きている」という評論を執筆しました。彼女は戦争が終わっても右翼とファシズムのイデオロギーは未だに克服されていないと認識していて、誤った安心感の下に眠っていてはいけないと呼びかけます。これこそ私たちが今立ち戻らなければならないものだと考えて

WVO：はい、そしていまやイタリアではムッソリーニのファシズムを悪びれもせず賞賛する者が当選しそうです。

いるので、新作のキャストには今日のファシズムについて話し合ってもらいます。芙美子の文章はそれとは異なるもので、今日のジェンダーやセクシュアリティと共鳴するものを与えてくれます。彼女は欲望に対してとても開かれた態度で執筆していました。

AM：各作品ではどのようにキャストと仕事をしていますか。《オブサダ》ではかなり協働的なアプローチを採用していたようでしたが、事前に入念に演出内容を準備することもあるのでしょうか。

撮影の準備段階でキャストと演出内容をたくさん話し合うことは一貫しています。作品を実現する上で、キャストの主体性や知識は重要ですから、自分たちがどんなものを制作しているのか、なぜ制作しているのかについて理解しておいてもらいたいと考えています。

撮影自体は、自分が撮りたいシーンはかなり入念に準備することが多く、たとえば、《オブサダ》の場合も二人組になったキャストに、歩きながらこの映画学校に入学した理由を話し合うように指示し、実際にそうしてもらいました。もちろん私は彼女たちがどんな話をするのか事前には知りません。彼女たちが非常にオープンに話し合い、互いに対する関心をとても純粋に抱いたことには本当に驚きました。一方、それとは異なる即興の可能性も残されていました。コブロの彫刻のガラスの台座への応答の他に、色付きのアクリル板を使うという案も協働的な対話を通じて生まれてきました。誰かひとりの手に状況を委ねるのではなく、出来上がるイメージの責任をみんなで引き受ける状況を作り出せないか。そのアイデアを考えてみようと、キャストに呼びかけました。あの色付きのアクリル板は、さまざまなイメージを共に作り出すための装置になりました。

実は新作についても面白い話があります。《ふたつの石》に出演したマヤはウクライナ人の翻訳家で、

WvO：プロジェクト毎に異なりますが、

同作のロケ地でロッテ・スタム＝ベーゼが共同設計したＫｈＴＺの集合住宅に暮らしています。来日前に話をした時に、東京で建築家として働いている友人がいるから会ってみたらどうかと勧めてくれました。その友人とはＫｈＴＺ育ちのヴェロニカという女性で、彼女は日本を代表する建築家のひとりである限研吾の事務所で働いていたのです。なんという巡り合わせでしょうか。ここでＫｈＴＺ出身の誰かに会えるなんて思いもしませんでした。さらに、彼女は修士課程で伝統的な日本建築について学んでいたので、芙美子の邸宅を「読む」こともできます。私たちが戸外から撮影する間、彼女には室内を移動しながらその要素を分析してもらいます。

ＡＭ：新作に出演した他のメンバーにはどんな人がいますか。どんなふうに芙美子と百合子に対する理解を助けてくれるのでしょうか。

ＷｖＯ：この作品で私たちが取り上げる問題に対して、各々がそれぞれの入り口を持っています。たとえば、黒澤亜里子は宮本百合子と湯浅芳子の往復書簡を調べ、彼女たちの日記を研究していますが、二〇〇八年に出版した著作では、二人の恋愛を当時の政治状況から論じています。ソコロワ山下聖美とグレッグ・ドボルザークの対話も撮影します。ソコロワ山下は文芸研究家で、林芙美子が戦時に従軍し、日本軍政下の各地、とりわけインドネシアを旅した時に執筆したものを研究しており、グレッグは東京を拠点に太平洋地域、その植民地性、ジェンダー、さまざまな権力による統治の歴史を研究しています。みんなで林芙美子の初期作やインドネシアに関連するものの一部、また、宮本百合子が同性愛関係にあった頃の日記や手紙に加えて、彼女の政治的な文章も読むつもりです。それらのテキストについて、五つくらいの焦点をめぐる読書や話し合いが行われる予定で、十一人のキャストの組み合わせを変えながら三つのロケ地で撮影

する予定です。最終的にどのような形になるのか私自身もまだわかりませんが、関連し合う要素はたくさんありますし、編集を進めながら鍵となるものを探っていきたいと思います。

AM：制作における建築の役割について話を戻します。あなたは映像内で建築空間を扱うだけでなく、展示空間にもしばしば建築的な介入を試みています。それは階段状になった独特な客席であったり、映画館のような設えであったり、たとえば、《ふたつの石》を初めて発表したベルリンの世界文化の家（HKW）では、鑑賞者が座る急角度のスロープを建てていました。あれは鑑賞者に不安定な感覚をもたらしたのではないかと想像しました。

WvO：世界文化の家では、メインの展示ホールにスクリーンを吊りましたが、主な鑑賞位置がバルコニーになるので、バルコニーの手すりの上からスクリーンを見るために、鑑賞者の位置も高くしなければなりませんでした。ただスロープをできる限り高くしたいと考えていたので、不安定な感覚を生むという効果は意図していませんでしたが、そんなことも時にはありますよね。実際、世界文化の家では作品に対する複数の体験の形がありました。バルコニーに座っていた人々は音も聴こえるし、映像を字幕と一緒に見られるので作品内のテキストの要素と自分を結びつけることができました。また、映像のみであれば他の位置からも見ることができました。結果的に面白い二段階の構造が生み出され、以降、この作品を展示する機会にはそれを繰り返すようになりました。

AM：東京都現代美術館の展示プランについて教えてもらえますか。

WvO：東京都現代美術館での建築的な介入も《オブサダ》の撮影のセットと同じようにかなりセンセーショ

ナルなものになると思います。基本的には展示空間に多角形を描くように連なるパーテーションを設置して、小さな空間をたくさん作る予定です。パーテーションには窓があるものや引き戸になっているものがあり、鑑賞者が自分で開けられるようになっているので、展示会場を移動しながらさまざまな枠を通して見ていくことになります。つまり、各作品がそれぞれ異なる開口部に縁取られる「登場人物」になるわけです。また、鑑賞者が座る段々になったプラットフォームは登ったり降りたりすることもできますし、本来の展示空間の一角がかなり狭い通路になるといった、通常はそこにないような変な空間もあったりします。このような建築的な介入は、美術館における普段の身体感覚に変化をもたらします。また書籍などいろいろなものが置かれた共有空間もあり、たとえばクィアやフェミニズムに関する読書会を開催することもできます。

今回、私はこの「建築」自体を作品だと捉えています。（映像作品の展示で一般的な）暗い部屋からその次の部屋へとただ移動するのとは異なり、鑑賞者は移動しながら、さまざまな空間や時間を体験することになるでしょう。

AM：展示空間への介入はただ映像作品を見せるということだけでなく、鑑賞者の主体性に対する関心から生まれているということですね。

WvO：私は以前からずっと鑑賞者を作品における積極的な参加者として考えてきました。作品と鑑賞者の間だけでなく、鑑賞者も展示空間でお互いに見えている存在なので、鑑賞者の間にも、さまざまな関係性を生み出したいと考えています。誰もがみな舞台上でのそれぞれのあり方を持っています。それは覗き見的なものとは違って、ある構図の中に自分の立ち位置を得るということです。鑑賞者には、自分自身の空

間と思考プロセスを持ってほしいと思っています。鑑賞者に作品から自分なりに何かを見出すよう促すレヒトの演劇みたいですが、私はそれをただ思考のレベルだけでなく、身体的なレベルでも求めているので、建築がとても重要になるのです。

AM：日本でリサーチし、プロジェクトを行ってみてどうでしたか。少しの間、少なくとも冒頭で私が挙げた地理的な繋がりの中に新たな場が加わるというようなことはありましたか。また、あなたの思考や作品制作に対する何か新しい気づきはもたらされたのでしょうか。

WvO：私と日本との関係は、二〇一六年のあいちトリエンナーレに招待されたことで始まりました。その時、自分が日本語で十まで数えられることを急に思い出してびっくりしました。それは私にとって子どもの頃に母が教えてくれた童謡のようなもので、突然記憶が戻ってきたのです。母は幼い頃、一九三〇年代から一九四〇年代にインドネシアに暮らしていた多くのオランダ国籍を持つ白人と共に、日本軍のジャワにある捕虜収容所に収容されていました。日本が侵略してきた一九四二年当時の母の年齢は八歳で、十二歳の時に解放されたのですが、それ以降はオランダで生活を送り、教育を受けました。おそらく彼女は朝の体操で、あのような数の数え方を学んだのではないでしょうか。そう、ある植民地支配層の生活が別の植民地支配層によって終止符を打たれたわけです。私はなぜか、この母の過去にまつわる記憶を自分が日本に招待された喜びと結び付けることはありませんでした。そう言えばそんなことがあったな、と。

日本に滞在して制作する中で気づいたのは、オランダとインドネシアと日本の間のもつれた三角関係に向けられる眼差しは、国家という単位での政治、痛み、誇りにより方向付けられたり、曖昧なものにされがちであるということです。オランダからアジアに向けられる眼差しが意味するものについてはかなり意

105　　　　　　　　　　　　ウェンデリン・ファン・オルデンボルフ：

識してきましたが、いまや日本からそれがいかに異なって見えるのかということに、より意識を向けています。その眼差しは異なる痛みや誇り、恥で組織され、その他のものを見えにくくしています。

私たちの認識を脱植民地化しようとする努力でさえ、学びほぐそうとする諸問題に内包されている「国家的なもの」に影響されるのは間違いありません。これもまた障害なんだということがどんどん見えてくるようになりました。そこで次のような問いが残されています。現在進行中の巨大なパラダイムシフト、それに伴う暴力を認識するアートの方法論とはどんなものだろうか。そして、このような価値観の変化を、この世界で共に生きていく上でよりバランスの取れた方向に導くために、私たちの作品に何ができるだろうか。私はしばしばベンジャミン・モーザーの書いたブラジルの小説家クラリッセ・リスペクトルの伝記の題名を思い出すのです。『なぜこの世界？』——この問いが全てを物語っていますね。

（展覧会ブックレットに、本インタビューの短縮版を掲載）

アンドリュー・マークル
アートライター、エディター、翻訳家。『ArtAsiaPacific』副編集長を経て、現在は『ART』「インターナショナル版」副編集長を務める。『Artforum』『frieze』などに寄稿。主な翻訳に、フー・ファン（中英）や田中功起の執筆（和英）。主な出版物に、菅木志雄論集の英訳版（第一巻、Skira、二〇二一年）。東京藝術大学大学院国際芸術創造研究科非常勤講師。

Film still from *Maurits Script*

《ヒア》映像スチル

Film still from *Hier.*

《彼女たちの》映像スチル

Film still from of girls

〈ふたつの石〉映像スチル

Film still from Two Stones

〈オブサダ〉映像スチル

Film still from obsada

Production still from of girls

《ヒア》映像スチル

Film still from *Hier*.

作品リスト・解説

マウリッツ・スクリプト ———— 116

偽りなき響き ———— 118

ふたつの石 ———— 120

ヒア ———— 122

オブサダ ———— 124

彼女たちの ———— 126

脚注：オブサダ（二〇二二年）
レンチキュラープリント（二枚組）120 × 180 cm

脚注：彼女たちの（二〇二二年）
レンチキュラープリント（二枚組）120 × 300 cm

マウリッツ・スクリプト（二〇〇六年）

構造物と冊子を含む2チャンネル映像インスタレーション

26分／38分

朗読、対話

アントニー・クラーク：アーティスト、仕立屋、デニム裁断師

ロメオ・K・ガンビエ：DJ、ラジオMC

シャロ・ランドフルフト：アーティスト、現代美術理論家、講師

ユニス・ランドフルフト：看護師、在宅ケアラー

クリスチャナ・デ・モライシュ・スミス：理論物理学者

ペーター・オルストホーン：政治学者、ライター、講師

ニンケ・テルプスマ：アーティスト、グラフィックデザイナー

アレクサンダー・フォラブレヒト：都市計画専門家、講師

撮影：ヨリス・ケルボス、サル・クローネンベルフ

録音：マタイン・ファン・ハーレン

撮影地：マウリッツハイス美術館（ハーグ、オランダ）

製作：カスコ・ユトレヒト

本作はオランダでは見過ごされがちな、ブラジル北東部にあった旧オランダ領ブラジルの歴史を起点とする。脚本は一六三七年から一六四四年まで総督を務めたヨハン・マウリッツ・ファン・ナッサウの人物像に基づいている。ファン・オルデンボルフは、オランダでは人道主義的な支配者として評価されているマウリッツの書簡や政治会議の議事録など、複数の一次資料をもとに脚本を構成した。それは、ポルトガル人とオランダ人の植民地入植者の間の紛争や、奴隷や先住民の扱いに関わるマウリッツの統治について知られてこなかった側面を複雑に描き出す。

タイトルが示すように、本作は脚本制作に関するものである。より具体的には、政治的、思想的な困難を避けることなく、複数の声と経験を体現することを目指す。ファン・オルデンボルフは、本作が取り上げる問題に異なる関係や立場を取る人々を、撮影の参加者として招待した。彼らが共に過去の言葉を読み解くことは、受け継がれてきた声について批評的に考察し、他の声をもたらす契機となる。

本作の撮影は、ハーグにあるマウリッツの旧居、マウリッツハイス美術館のゴールデンルームで一日限りの公開イベントとして行われた。部屋の片側では、参加者が個々に文献を読み、もう片側では、他の参加者がテーブルを囲んで会話する。そこでは、現在のオランダ社会、特にその公民権や多文化主義のあり方に根付く植民地時代の遺産について、時に相反する視点が提示されながら議論が交わされる。この対話は一日を通して勢いを増し、カメラクルーや観客を巻き込みながら広がっていく。

偽りなき響き（二〇〇八年）

映像インスタレーション
二枚の音響パネルを含む
30分

声、出演

サラ・エディーン：オランダ社会の移民排除に関する問題をテーマに、オランダ語とアラビア語で歌うラッパー。オランダの政治家ヘルト・ファン・ウィルダースは、二〇〇八年に発表した映画『フィトナ』で、エディーンの写真を、映画監督テオ・ファン・ゴッホを殺害したモハンマド・ボウイェリと誤って使用した。

エドウィン・ユリエンス：ニューサウスウェールズ大学講師。著書に『独白から対話へ・インドネシアのラジオと改革』（二〇一〇年、未訳）などがある。ラジオをはじめとするインドネシアのポピュラーメディアとグローバル化の関係について研究する。

ウィム・ノルドフック：ラジオプロデューサー、ジャーナリスト、文筆家。一九六七年以来、オルタナティブ・ミュージックを放送する番組を定期的に制作。二〇〇〇年にはオランダの公共放送VPRO（自由主義プロテスタントラジオ放送の略）で、フィリップス・コンサーン・アーカイブがレコード盤に保存していたオリジナルの収録を用いて、PHOHI（オランダ領東インド・フィリップス放送局）に関する一連の番組を制作した。

バウヴェ・プリンス：ハーグ応用科学大学准教授、専門はオランダにおける市民権と多様性。著書に『ビヨンド・イノセンス：オランダにおける統合についての論争』（二〇〇四年、未訳）、『偶然のクラスメイト：人種、階級、ジェンダーと宗教が交差する生の話』（二〇一四年、未訳）など。

ヨス・ウィビソノ：一九八七年から勤務するラジオ・ネーデルランド（元オランダの国営国際放送局）のインドネシア部門編集長。バリやジャワの伝統音楽であるガムランが西洋音楽に与えた影響を中心に、オランダとインドネシアの関係を専門に研究している。スワルディ・スルヤニングラットについて博士論文を執筆した。

リナ・カンパネッラ：国立青少年合唱団で訓練中の歌手、撮影当時八歳。

撮影：ヨリス・ケルボス、ミヒャエル・ブルック
録音：ルド・エンゲルス、ピーター・キュー
撮影地：ラジオ・コートワイク（アーペルドールン、オランダ）

製作：ファン・アッベ美術館

作品リスト・解説

ヨーロッパでは、ラジオは演説や講義を通じて大衆を教育する国家統制の道具として発展した。

本作は、こうしたラジオの歴史、特に旧オランダ領東インド（現在のインドネシア）におけるラジオについて振り返る。オランダの電気機器メーカー、フィリップス社は一九二〇年代後期、植民地に向け、ラジオ技術を輸出するだけでなく番組も制作した。その目的は、無邪気で高揚感ある内容で、望ましくない政治的な声を排除することにあった。十二月の聖ニコラウスの祝祭に関する番組などを通じて、支配者側のオランダ人たちは郷愁や安らぎを抱いた一方、インドネシアの人々は民族主義的な自己認識を形成していった。現代オランダの国家主義的感情の再燃を背景に制作された本作は、上記の歴史から、同時に興っていた相反するナショナリズムの動向に着目している。

本作の舞台となったのは、近代的発展を象徴する記念碑的な建築物であり、旧オランダ領東インドに初めて無線電信を送った放送局ラジオ・コートワイクの旧本館である。かつての機能を失い、長らく放置されてきたこの場所で撮影された本作を構成するのは、ラジオ番組のごとく、即興的でも探求的でもなく、断定的で教訓的とも言える声である。映像は二人の歴史家と、現在の政治的傾向を分析する専門家がオランダ側の視点について議論する様子を捉える。その一方で、インドネシア独立運動家の声は、一九一三年に発刊された冊子に掲載された記事「もし私がオランダ人であったなら」によって象徴される。独立運動家スワルディ・スルヤニングラットによるこの挑発的なマニフェストは、モロッコ系オランダ人のラッパー、サラ・エディーンによって朗読される。彼は現代オランダ社会での移民の扱いを痛烈に批判してきた人物でもある。彼らの他に観客を招いて撮影された本作では、歴史資料の扱いを引用しながら、現在の問題について自発的に会話する人々の様子も捉えている。

　　　　　　　　　　　　　　　　偽りなき響き

ふたつの石 （二〇一九年）

2チャンネルの音声と字幕を
含むシングルチャンネル映像
インスタレーション
各28分

対話・出演
ハンナ・ドーン・ヘンダーソン：アーティスト、ライター。ハーグ（オランダ）拠点。
イヴジェニア・グブキナ：建築家、アクティビスト、ライター。ハルキウ（ウクライナ）拠点。
マヤ・スモルニャニノヴァ：翻訳家。ハルキウ拠点。
オラ・ハサネイン：アーティスト、建築家。ユトレヒト（オランダ）及びハルツーム（スーダン）拠点。
ハネケ・オースターホフ：ロッテ・スタム＝ベーゼの伝記作家。ウーンスドレヒト（オランダ）拠点。

ロマン・ブデスキヴ
ソフィア・ディボック
アンドリィ・フレップニコウ
ディミトロ・ブラク
ナタリア・ドロシュク
ヨランダ・レンフルム

撮影：マシャ・オームス
録音：リック・マイアー
整音：ティトゥス・マデレヒュナ
撮影地：ハルキウ・トラクター工場（KhTZ）、ベンドレヒト地区（ロッテルダム、オランダ）
製作：ファビアン・アルテンリード（シュルデンベルグ・フィルムズ）
協力：バウハウス・イマジニスタ

本作は、バウハウスで学んだドイツ人建築家ロッテ・スタム＝ベーゼと、カリブ出身のアクティビストで文筆家のヘルミナ・ハウスヴァウトの軌跡と理想を、現代を生きる登場人物たちによる対話から探る。スタム＝ベーゼもハウスヴァウトも、一九三〇年代初期にソビエト連邦で活動し、第二次世界大戦後はオランダで活躍した。本作の撮影は、スタム＝ベーゼが一九三〇年代に、ウクライナのハルキウ・トラクター工場（ＫhＴＺ）で初めて手がけたロシア構成主義建築による集合住宅地と、一九五〇年代、ロッテルダム（オランダ）の主要建築家・都市計画家として設計したペンドレヒトという住宅地で行われた。ハウスヴァウトは一九七〇年代、ペンドレヒトを含むロッテルダム全ての地区において、カリブ系オランダ人が人口の五パーセントを超えてはならないという住宅法に対する抗議運動を行っていた。これらに個人的、または職業的に関係する現代の登場人物たちの経験や考察からは、二人の軌跡と、それぞれが抱いていた社会主義思想の共鳴と不協和が見て取れる。

二〇一八年に撮影された本作では二つの場所が重なり合い、空間的な相似点をリズミカルに提示する。イメージを重ねたひとつの映像に二種類の音声を組み合わせた多層的な本作のインスタレーションでは、この二つの地域に結び付けられたスティグマと隔離という概念もまた呼応する。

ヒア（二〇二一年）

木枠を含む4チャンネル・ビデオウォール
27分

テキスト、対話、音楽、出演
ベルミ・アデジュモ：小説家、詩人、劇作家。作品中で朗読しているテキストは、彼女が本作のために書き下ろしたもの。
ララ・ヌーベルグ：オランダとインドネシアの植民地時代の歴史について執筆、発表する研究者。

FREDメンバー：
リヤナ・ウサ：リード・ギタリストでシンガーソングライター。デルフト工科大学で電子工学を専攻。
ジョセフィーヌ・スピット：ベーシスト。デルフト工科大学で建築学を専攻。
ティルザ・ヒワット：ドラマーでマルチプレイヤー。ユトレヒト大学で情報科学を専攻。

撮影：ローレンス・リー・カルクマン
録音：ルール・ボトホーヴェン
整音：タイラー・フリードマン
撮影地：改修工事中のアーネム美術館（アーネム、オランダ）

共同製作：ハンナ・ドーン・ヘンダーソン
協力：ソンスベーク20→24

この作品では、複数の叙情的表現と声が結びつきを成し、個人の記憶と政治的省察を行き来する。

映像には、改修工事中のアーネム美術館（オランダ）——変移する保存の場——を舞台に、音楽、詩、対話を通して自らを表現する若い女性たちが登場する。彼女たちは異種混交性、トランスナショナル、ディアスポラといったテーマに繊細に触れながら、植民地時代の歴史の余韻が未だに根強い現代において、「アイデンティティ」や「文化の刷新」が政治的に利用される傾向について語る。

本作においては、場所もまた重要な「声」である。アーネム美術館は元々、十九世紀後期、権威あるフロート・ソシエタイトの会員になる社会的地位に至らないアーネム市民が設立した紳士クラブであった。彼らの多くは、オランダ植民地との繋がりがある人々でもあった。映像では、建物の基礎だけが残され、古いコンクリート構造に優雅なアール・ヌーヴォーの特徴が見て取れる。過去の瓦礫と未来の可能性が対照を織りなす場所に、三つの「音脈」が響く。バンド「FRED」がインドネシアの伝統的なクロンチョン音楽を即興で演奏した後、彼女らの現代的な歌を演奏する。ペルミ・アデジュモは他のキャストとの対話の後に書いたテキストを朗読し、ララ・ヌーベルグはさまざまな資料、声明、音楽、建物に応答してゆく。彼女たちの音楽と詩は社会政治的な問題だけでなく、自らの存在に対する問いや、彼女たちが感じている弱さを底流に湛えている。柔らかでありながら自信に満ち、互いに友情と思いやりを示す出演者たちは、愛とそれに伴う悲しみ、人生における疑問と確信について語りながら、未来に変化を与えうる原動力を表現する。

オブサダ（二〇二一年）

シングルチャンネル映像
インスタレーション
34分

対話、出演
マグダレナ・ポジド：撮影監督。ワルシャワ（ポーランド）拠点。
パウリナ・サシャ：録音監督、助産師。ワルシャワ及びベルリン（ドイツ）拠点。
モニカ・チャイコフスカ：監督、脚本家、プロデューサー・講師。ワルシャワ拠点。
エヴァ・ポリシヴィッチ：監督、脚本家、ビジュアル・アーティスト。ワルシャワ拠点。
マグダ・クップリヤノヴィッチ：劇作家、脚本家。ワルシャワ拠点。
エルズビエタ・スルピカ：衣装デザイナー、舞台デザイナー。ワルシャワ拠点。
アレクサンドラ・ロゼット：編集者。ウッチ（ポーランド）拠点。
ジョアンナ・ソコロウスカ：キュレーター。ウッチ拠点。

撮影：マグダレナ・ポジド
録音：パウリナ・サシャ
撮影地：ウッチ美術館、ウッチ映画大学（ウッチ、ポーランド）

共同製作：ヤコブ・ダニレヴィッチ、モニカ・チャイコフスカ
製作・協力：ウッチ美術館、ウッチ映画大学ヴァーチャル・ナラティブ研究室、モンドリアン財団

作品リスト・解説

本作のタイトル「オブサダ」(obsada)は、ポーランド語で「キャスト」、「共同作業」、「植物を植える」など複数の意味を持つ。撮影では、ウッチ(ポーランド)にある国立映画大学の女性の学生や卒業生、プロの撮影クルーが、映画大学とウッチ美術館で互いを撮影しながら、女性という立場から映画制作について話し合った。この二つの機関は、彼女たちの対話に歴史的な参照点や文脈を提示している。そのひとつに、ロシア構成主義に影響を受けた、全員男性の前衛グループ「ワークショップ・オブ・ザ・フィルム・フォルム」(一九七〇—一九七七年)がある。このグループは当時の映画大学の学生やアーティストたちが伝統的な教育を批判し、映画と現代美術の橋渡しをすることを目的に設立した。彼らは一九七三年、ウッチ美術館で、映画撮影術、制作、オーサーシップの拡張や芸術教育に関する彼らの思想を実践するため、「ワークショップ・アクション」と題された二十三日間のイベントを開催した。

本作のキャストと撮影クルーは、ファン・オルデンボルフと協働し撮影をする過程で、一連の即興的なアクションを行った。それらは、「ワークショップ・オブ・ザ・フィルム・フォルム」や、特定の視点を定めない無限空間の具体的表現を目指した構成主義の女性彫刻家カタジナ・コブロ(一八九八—一九五一年)に触発されたものであった。彼女たちはそういったアクションを通じて、初期の前衛運動が問題にせず、今もなお存在する家父長的な特権が、芸術分野で活動する自らの主観性や切望の形成に深く影響していることについて率直に話し合った。本作における女性たちの声と一連のアクションは、すでに起きた変化と、未だもたらされていない変化を示唆すると同時に、制作活動における協働と開放性とは何かを体現している。

オブサダ

彼女たちの
（二〇二二年）

シングルチャンネル映像
インスタレーション
40分

朗読、対話

アリウェン：アーティスト、キュレーター、ライター、東京拠点。

グレッグ・ドボルザーク：アーティスト、ライター、研究者。専門は太平洋とアジアの歴史学、ジェンダー・スタディーズ、ポストコロニアル・スタディーズ。著書に『珊瑚とコンクリート：日本、アメリカ、マーシャル諸島におけるワジェリン環礁の記憶』（二〇一八年、未訳）。東京拠点。

平河伴菜：アーティスト、キュレーター。東京藝術大学大学院国際芸術創造研究科在籍。東京拠点。

ヴェロニカ・イコンニコワ：アーティスト、建築家、東京拠点。

黒澤亜里子：近代日本・沖縄文学、フェミニズム文学、クィア理論研究者。編著に『往復書簡 宮本百合子と湯浅芳子』（二〇〇八年）。沖縄拠点。

チェルシー・センディ・シーダー：近現代のアクティビズム、ジェンダー・スタディーズ研究者。著書に『共学革命：一九六〇年代日本の新左翼と女子学生』（二〇二一年、未訳）。東京拠点。

ソコロワ山下聖美：近代日本文学研究者。著書に『林芙美子とインドネシア：作品と研究』（二〇二二年）。東京拠点。

田村万里子：東京都現代美術館学芸員。東京拠点。

谷川果菜絵：アーティスト、野良リサーチャー、アーティストデュオMES、FAQ?、NEON BOOK CLUBのメンバー。東京拠点。

イーチン：DJ、etherのオーガナイザー、NEON BOOK CLUBのメンバー。東京拠点。

横田実優：俳優、アーティスト・コレクティブ「ザ・フー」のメンバー。東京拠点。

引用テキスト

・林芙美子『蒼馬を見たり』日本図書センター、二〇〇一年。（英語版は『I Saw a Pale Horse and Selected Poems from Diary of a Vagabond』J・ブラウン訳、コーネル大学東アジアプログラム、一九九七年。）

・林芙美子『林芙美子 放浪記 復元版 廣畑研二編』論創社、二〇一一年。（英語版は『Be a Woman』ジョアン・E・エリクソン編、ハワイ大学出版局、一九九七年。）

・黒澤亜里子編、『往復書簡 宮本百合子と湯浅芳子』翰林書房、二〇〇八年。

・宮本百合子「ファシズムは生きている」「平和は眠りを許さない」新日本出版社、一九八九年。

・宮本百合子「乳房」、『宮本百合子選集 第三巻』新日本出版社、一九六八年。

撮影：飯岡幸子

撮影助手・照明：北川喜雄、村上拓也

録音：黄 永昌、藤口諒太

整音：藤口諒太

制作進行：大舘奈津子（一色事務所）

撮影地：林芙美子記念館、神奈川県立図書館、元映画館

製作・協力：東京都現代美術館、モンドリアン財団

東京と横浜で撮影された本作では、政治と文学の歴史に名を刻む二人の日本人女性と現代を生きる人々の声が共鳴する。一九二〇年代から人気を博し、共に一九五一年に夭逝した林芙美子（一九〇三―一九五一年）と宮本百合子（一八九九―一九五一年）は、優れた文才を持ち合わせ、女性や階級の問題に強い意識を持っていた。しかし、二人の生まれ育ちは大きく異なり、それぞれの生き方と理想の追求においても異なる道筋を描いた。

貧困家庭に生まれた林芙美子は、女性労働者への共感や自らの性的欲望を率直に表現した半自伝的な小説や詩で名を成し、東京都新宿区に自ら設計した自邸を建てた。一方、戦争中は、帝国陸軍や大手新聞社からの依頼でインドネシアを含む占領地に足を運び、さまざまな記事や詩を寄稿した。

宮本百合子は社会主義的理想と女性解放といった政治的信念を貫いた著作と生涯で知られている。恵まれた家庭で育った宮本はニューヨークへの留学後、日本人男性と結婚したが、ロシア文学研究者で作家であり、同性愛者であった湯浅芳子との出会いをきっかけに離婚。湯浅とは七年間の同棲生活を送り、その経験を複数の小説にした。その後、社会主義者である宮本顕治と結婚し、獄中の夫を幾度も投獄を経験した。

二人の言葉が内包する力強さと矛盾は、本作の舞台――文化、記憶、知識を象徴する諸空間――に登場する、異なる世代のキャストによる朗読や対話と共鳴し、今日におけるジェンダー、政治、情愛をめぐる葛藤を反映する。

展覧会

ウェンデリン・ファン・オルデンボルフ
柔らかな舞台

二〇二二年十一月十二日—二〇二三年二月十九日
東京都現代美術館企画展示室三階

主催：公益財団法人東京都歴史文化財団 東京都現代美術館
助成：モンドリアン財団、オランダ王国大使館

企画：崔 敬華（東京都現代美術館）
学芸補佐：田村万里子（東京都現代美術館）、平河伴菜、青木識至（インターン）
広報：工藤千愛子、内堀夢梨実、稲葉智子（東京都現代美術館）
会場設営・展示：HIGURE 17-15 cas

MUSEUM OF CONTEMPORARY ART TOKYO 東京都現代美術館

mondriaan fonds

Kingdom of the Netherlands

本展開催にあたり、多大なる協力を賜りました下記の諸機関、関係者の皆様に心より御礼申し上げます。（敬称略）

ウェンデリン・ファン・オルデンボルフ

モンドリアン財団、オランダ王国大使館

阿部航太、赤松立太、アリウェン、有元利彦、ビンナ・チョイ、ヤコブ・ダニレヴィッチ、パブロ・デ・オカンポ、グレッグ・ドボルザーク、江口愛美、藤口諒太、原田美緒、平河伴菜、黄永昌、ヴェロニカ・イコンニコワ、岩間朝子、菅野優香、北川喜雄、黒澤亜里子、アンドリュー・マークル、村上拓也、大舘奈津子、岡村忠征、良知暁、沢部仁美、チェルシー・センディ・シュナイダー、島内哲郎、清水知子、SHION、ソコロワ山下聖美、鈴木宏、竹花帯子、武市紀子、谷川果菜絵、うらあやか、若林亜希子、逸青、横田実優

株式会社キューブフィルム、エトセトラブックス、ザ・フー、新宿区立林芙美子記念館、神奈川県立図書館、元映画館、NEON BOOK CLUB、映画館ストレンジャー、すみだ向島EXPO、一色事務所

ウェンデリン・ファン・オルデンボルフ
柔らかな舞台

発行日　二〇二二年十二月二十八日　第一版

監修　東京都現代美術館

執筆　菅野優香、ビンナ・チョイ、パブロ・デ・オカンポ、アンドリュー・マークル、崔敬華

アートディレクション　若林亜希子

編集　柴原聡子、網野奈央 (torch press)

編集アシスタント　田村万里子、平河伴菜、青木識至、鳥屋菜々子 (torch press)

翻訳　マット・トライヴォー (EN pp. 23-33)、良知暁 (JP pp. 91-106)、片桐由賀 (JP pp. 43-58, 81 [略歴])、河野晴子 (JP pp. 67-81)、平河伴菜／崔敬華 (JP pp. 116-126)

英文校閲　リンゼイ・ウェストブルック (pp. 23-34, 91-106を除く)

会場撮影　森田兼次

印刷・製本　株式会社八紘美術

ISBN　978-4-907562-38-0

発行所　torch press
〒404-0054 山梨県甲州市塩山藤木一九五九
torchpress.net | order@torchpress.net

《彼女たちの》映像スチル

Film still from of girls

《ふたつの石》映像スチル

Film still from *Two Stones*

wendelien van oldenborgh

unset on-set

Table of contents

The fluid topos of Wendelien van Oldenborgh ___ 7
        Kyongfa Che

An opaque feminist/queer polyphony _____ 23
        Yuka Kanno

When we assemble _____ 43
        Binna Choi

An image of study _____ 67
        Pablo de Ocampo

Wendelien van Oldenborgh: An interview ___ 91
        Andrew Maerkle

List of works _____ 115

The fluid topos of Wendelien van Oldenborgh

Kyongfa Che

Curator, Museum of Contemporary Art Tokyo

Wendelien van Oldenborgh's multifaceted practice, spanning more than twenty years now, takes film production as a basis for generating forms of performativity that critique and deviate from dominant powers and discourses. The artist sets up a film shoot by choosing locations, materials, and people who participate as cast and crew, all of which relate to the area of interest or issue, and documents the conversations and other interactions that she facilitates and mediates. She then edits the footage into intricate entanglements of the participants' subjectivities and social relations, offering multiplicities of perspectives and sensitivities on the issue they engage.

Van Oldenborgh first experimented with film production in *A Certain Brazilianness* (2004–2008), which she organized upon moving back to the Netherlands after living in various countries, and building strong personal ties with Brazil in particular. The central aim was to create settings where people form and negotiate relations without necessarily orchestrating harmony, counterposing Brazil's Modernist movement and other cultural strategies valorizing difference against an imagined, unified national identity. Over the course of several events, a group of participants fluidly exchanged the positions and roles of performers and audience in hip-hop jam sessions, talks, and other social interactions that were recorded and shared with the public. The two-screen film installation presented in this exhibition, *Maurits Script* (2006), was produced at one stage in this long-term project, which opened up new horizons for Van Oldenborgh's film production.

In *Maurits Script*, people from various backgrounds gather for a one-day public film shoot at Mauritshuis museum in the Hague. They revisit historical materials Van Oldenborgh assembled on Johan Maurits van Nassau, governor of 17th-century Dutch Brazil, and interrogate the historiographies

and legacies of colonial power abiding in contemporary Dutch society. In the final work, one of the two screens shows participants reading the words of the related historical figures by reciting fragments of archival texts, while the other shows conversations in which they bring forward their own experiences, knowledge, and emotional realities of living in the Netherlands. The camera often focuses on subtle gestures and nuanced expressions as participants speak or listen intently to others. It also captures in-between moments and random happenings spurred by those who are in or out of the "frame" in the conventional sense, such as museum visitors encountering the film shoot, Van Oldenborgh intervening in the discussions, or film crews at work with booms, cameras, and makeup kits, constituting an intriguing interplay between control and spontaneity.

As in other works by Van Oldenborgh, the cinematography and editing are less concerned with cinematic consistency than the opposite; via self-reflexive, overlooking long shots, erratic ruptures, and extreme close-ups, linear narratives and indexical representations are avoided. The artist relentlessly reveals the deed of constructing a situation (in this case a film shoot) and how one, whether the artist or a member of the cast or crew, acts, speaks, or listens within it and constitute a temporal constellation of social relations and discourse, while bringing our attention to performativity. And it is here that Van Oldenborgh seeks the potentiality of transformation. As she once put it: "It is the practice toward finding and shaping alternative structures in thinking, in perceiving, in interpreting, in appreciating, and in constructing. This work will never be formatted or fixed in one particular way but always be shifting according to the time in which it is functioning." [1]

1   Wendelien van Oldenborgh, "The Work We Do," *Amateur* (Berlin: Sternberg Press; London: The Showroom, 2014), 373.

The title the artist and I settled on for this exhibition, *unset on-set*, alludes to the affective register of her work. It unsettles rather than consolidates, interrogates rather than asserts, the conditions and frameworks we live in, which also reflects Van Oldenborgh's intention to create a large installation that evokes the idea of a stage, inter-locating the bodies, gazes, and voices in the works and their audiences. The works presented in the installation, *Maurits Script*, *No False Echoes* (2008), *Two Stones* (2019), *Hier.* (2021), *obsada* (2021), and a new work, *of girls* (2022), all demonstrate Van Oldenborgh's continuous exploration of filmic methodology and engagement with colonialism, nationalism, patriarchy, and gender. The selection of existing works was based on our conversations regarding how these issues intersect and affect our distant yet connected histories and societies today. Our exchanges also motivated the production of a new work that draws such intersections within the Japanese context.

When we started our regular online communications in spring 2021, Van Oldenborgh had recently produced *Hier.* in the Netherlands and was preparing for the next pro-duction of *obsada* in Poland. Both involve women in cultural and academic fields probing various aspects of their identities and vulnerabilities through music, poetry, and dialogue, seeking alternative modalities of articulating their subjectivities. "The new voice is already there," Van Oldenborgh once told me. The voice attempts to crack open the gap to emancipate itself from existing forces embedded in norms, discourses, and language.

Filmed in Tokyo and Yokohama in autumn 2022, *of girls* summons reverberations of voices from the past and present that address women's negotiations and struggles regarding their positions in society. Eleven cast members hailing from different generations and geographies, with various

gender orientations and professions, read fragments of essays, poems, and fictional novels by two notable Japanese women writers of the 20th century, Fumiko Hayashi and Yuriko Miyamoto, who both lived through the tumultuous war years but from vastly different positions and political attitudes. Openly but carefully, the cast spells out their empathies, dissents and ambivalences as they contextualize the writers' struggles and aspirations based on their own experiences and speculations. In the collective engagement with the texts across different subjects, styles, and languages (Japanese and English), multiplicities of inter-subjective dynamics are generated and appear as resonances or subtly dissonant tensions. As is suggested by Van Oldenborgh's visual experiment of collapsing time and space by juxtaposing two frames that keep panning, we see in the assemblage of fragmented conversations gaps and differences (re)formulating between texts/ speakers and the cast/listeners, and among the cast who then becomes speakers to potential listeners. Reminding us that differences are laid open to ethical and political negotiation within, as much as in between, subjects, the heterogeneities harbored in this piece pose questions of agency, such as how we reconcile the unknowable and the untranslatable, or how we perceive unbridgeable gaps as distance or proximity. Van Oldenborgh invites us into a fluid topos where we exercise these gaps in defining and redefining our selves and formulating relations.

I would like to convey my deepest gratitude to Wendelien van Oldenborgh, who committed so much energy to producing the exhibition and stayed in Tokyo for three months to take on the challenge of making her new work. I would also like to thank the cast, crew, and all others who so generously supported the artist's efforts. My sincere gratitude to Yuka Kanno, Binna Choi, and Pablo de Ocampo,

who shared remarkable insights through the texts they contributed, and to Andrew Maerkle for his engaging interview with the artist.

Installation view

So it's kind of... I feel like she is blaming
herself, because that's easier maybe.

An opaque feminist/ queer polyphony

Yuka Kanno

Translation by Matt Treyvaud

The work of Wendelien van Oldenborgh, in which speech and dialogue are the chief activities employed to create a cinematic world, has often been described as distinguished by its polyphony. Polyphony, which originally meant music in multiple voices, was conceptualized by Mikhail Bakhtin as the basic principle of Dostoevsky's poetics. Reconceived as a literary theory or artistic philosophy, it allows the possibility of "open" spaces in which authors and characters can engage in dialogue and multiple voices resound together without losing their autonomy. However, another important perspective for unraveling Oldenborghian polyphony is feminism, this being the critical practice that explores the possibilities of multiple coexisting readings while listening to multiple voices. Feminist critique resists uniformity and does not shy from rupture or inconsistency; it finds significance in the absence of consistency and places value in ambiguity. It is an attempt to read the conflicts and tensions between women in places where the meanings of words and images sideslip, derail, and are pluralized.

Van Oldenborgh's feminist polyphony is supported by a style and aesthetic centered around movement, fragmentation, and opacity. Points of view are slowly transformed by constant unhurried camera movement. Fragmentary shots interrupt the flow abruptly, like a rejection of smoothness itself. Opaque images that guide the gaze to surfaces while laying materiality bare possess a depth impenetrable to vision. These opaque images, which appear accompanied by cinematography that literally "writes with movement" and editing that emphasizes and fragments the autonomy of the shot, are the crux of an Oldenborghian cinematic world that distances itself from clarity, continuity, and visibility.

Van Oldenborgh's new work, *of girls* (2022), was conceived with women writers of modern Japan as its subject matter, and this project resonates with the attentiveness to *relationships between women* that runs through not only works featured at this exhibition like *Two Stones* (2019), *Hier.* (2021), and *obsada* (2021), but also middle-period works like *Bete & Deise* (2012). Van Oldenborgh's cinematic work has always been created through the act of reading texts, and this is reiterated in *of girls*. When Van Oldenborgh's characters read texts aloud not only vocally but also physically through a range of gestures and attitudes, past is fused with present, and meanings submerged in history resurface in the present as new meanings entirely.

The texts that intersect in *Two Stones*, for example, are the writings of activist Hermina Huiswoud and the places and structures upholding the memory of architect Lotte Stam-Beese's involvement in urban planning and public housing design. Memories of cities and buildings captured through various angles and frames rise, called up by the diverse "voices" of people living in the present day. When text and text come into contact, violating each other's boundaries and blending together, the multiplicity of layers and voices renders them opaque.

In *Hier.*, texts constructed of multiple media, including writing and music, come into contact and resonate with each other. However, while the multi-textual intersections that arise as a result are presented accompanied by leisurely movements, they are never smoothly continuous. These texts, which speak of belonging and sexuality, are read aloud by a range of different women, despite lacking any clear objective due to rhythmic irregularity in the form of interruption, stagnation, and sudden acceleration. Also important is the fact that all this takes place in a museum

An opaque feminist/queer polyphony

under renovation. The camera captures the building's materiality in full, down to the smallest details of construction and materials; it is an Oldenborghian space, which makes contact between past and present possible.

of girls, which explores the particularity in experiences that arise due to womanhood as well as the relationships that exist notwithstanding the ineradicable disparities between women, seems almost a variation on the feminist polyphony unintentionally exposed by *Bete & Deise*. In *Bete & Deise*, a chance encounter between two women re-examines the meaning of the political and broadens what it means to be political and the possibilities thereof. Actor Bete Mendes has been involved in many domestic political movements in Brazil, and is a "political woman" in the usual sense. Singer Deize Tigrona does not rely on any existing vocabulary for discussing politics and appears apolitical at a glance, but her woman-empowering lyrics and performances generate an unintentional political effect. The relationship between the two as they engage in dialogue goes from friendly to uneasy, and the work depicts the divergences and cracks in their relationship with care. The diversity within "being political" created by these two women who differ in class and race reflects the heterogeneity of, and expands the possibilities of, "woman" as a category.

The relationships between women foregrounded in Van Oldenborgh's work reveal themselves to be complex emotional connections, replete with inconsistencies, incapable of being fully captured by the idea of "bonds" or "solidarity" that are sometimes hinted at. The three women who are the focus of *of girls*, too, are clearly inscribed with the disparities that arise from differences in their individual experiences of womanhood. At the same time, the instability and opacity of womanhood as

an identity also becomes an opportunity to remake what it means to be a woman. Fumiko Hayashi started her career as a poet and became one of the Showa period's preeminent writers, with an oeuvre including works like *Diary of a Vagabond* (*Horoki*, 1928–1930) and *Floating Clouds* (*Ukigumo*, 1951); Yuriko Miyamoto debuted as a writer at 18 with *A Flock of Poor People* (*Mazushiki hitobito no mure*, 1916) and went on to become a pioneer in Japan's "proletarian literature" movement; Yoshiko Yuasa went from magazine journalist to translator of Russian literature. These three women, differing in both their relationship to literature and their origins, are summoned for an encounter in Van Oldenborgh's cinematic world.

The Literary Pull of Fumiko Hayashi

Why does Fumiko Hayashi call so strongly to other women writers? Beginning with the critical biography by contemporary Taiko Hirabayashi and continuing into the present, countless women writers have succumbed to the literary pull of Fumiko Hayashi. Natsuo Kirino, the writer who has most incisively penetrated the adversity faced by women in contemporary society, used Fumiko Hayashi as the model for her novel *Something's There* (*Nanika aru*, 2010), a mixture of invention and history in which she reimagines the question "What happened down south?", referring to Southeast Asia during the Pacific War.[1] Rieko Matsuura, whose experimental novels about female eros and relationships between women raise new questions about the normativity of gender and sexuality, also evokes Fumiko Hayashi in her *Opposite Version* (*Ura bajon*, 2000). In this

1   Ayako Sakuma argues that *Something's There* was written in order to unravel the mystery of the creation of *Floating Clouds*, Hayashi's finest work. Ayako Sakuma, "Kaisetsu" [Afterword], in Natsuo Kirino, *Nanika aru* [Something's There] (Shincho Bunko, Tokyo: Shinchosha, 2012), 585.

novel, which depicts a queer relationship between two women, short story writer Masako "speaks of her past as a failed writer" in what is, according to Yuko Iida, a parody of *Diary of a Vagabond*.[2] If we take inversion and repetition based on critical distance to be parody, then the critical distance *Opposite Version* adopts with respect to *Diary of a Vagabond* is surely the fact of writing a novel as a woman, or of being conscious of how and to whom a woman as a writing subject relates an autobiographical novel based on her own experience. Furthermore, the autobiographical nature of *Diary of a Vagabond* depends not on whether it is fact or fiction but in its stubborn questioning of ways of being a woman as a social subject, transcending Hayashi's individual experiences. Maiko Odaira, who calls *Diary of a Vagabond* "a strange edifice that was repeatedly enlarged," says that this novel is autobiographical not because it is grounded in fact but because Hayashi weaves into it her long years of negotiating the circumstances surrounding women.[3]

Hayashi continued updating *Diary of a Vagabond* until her death, and a powerful self-awareness of being a woman runs through her intentions toward the writing subject; her own womanhood is inextricably connected to society. The women writers of today's Japan seem to respond to Hayashi's vacillation around the position of women, and see their own survival in that struggle. And now, along with *of girls*, we are about to become readers of Fumiko Hayashi once more. The Fumiko Hayashi we meet anew here is a woman who not only depicted the illusion of a Japan bloated by

2   The novel is built around a queer relationship between two middle-aged women who were friends in high school. It is made up of 18 chapters in the form of short stories written by one woman and harsh commentary from the other. Yuko Iida, *Kanojotachi no bungaku: Katarinikusa to yomareru koto* [The literature of women: The difficulty of speaking, and being read] (Nagoya: The University of Nagoya Press, 2016).

3   Maiko Odaira, "Hayashi Fumiko: Sekirara no saji kagen—*Horoki* no kakikae wo megutte" [Hayashi Fumiko: Outspokenness and discretion —On the rewriting of *Diary of a Vagabond*] *Waseda bungaku zokan joseigo*, No. 1026 (2017), 402.

4   For example, regarding the question of why *Floating Clouds* is considered Hayashi's greatest work in the current history of its study, Saori Sakamoto observes that "the characters are thrown out to the water's edge of an 'expanding/shrinking Japan,' and the dynamism that arises there is depicted by replacing them with the concrete circumstances of men and women." Saori Sakamoto, "*Nanika aru* no 'kizuato': Senso/shokumin no 'kioku' to 'kiroku'" [The 'scars' of *Something's There*: 'Memories' and 'records' of war/colony] *Shiso*, No. 1159 (2020), 49.

imperialism by replacing them with "the circumstances of men and women" but also directed a queer gaze and desire at other women and included relationships between women rich in queer possibilities in the conditions for the formation of women as social subjects.[4] Hayashi spoke of sex with extreme directness, and this exhibition makes it clear that her range was not necessarily limited to heterosexuality.

To Be in Motion

One of the few points of commonality between Fumiko Hayashi, Yuriko Miyamoto, and Yoshiko Yuasa is *motion*—not just geographic dislocation, but social and psychic movement. Hayashi, who constructed a woman as a writing subject from the motion of vagabondage, began *Diary of a Vagabond* with the words "I am a vagabond by fate. I have no hometown," but even after this novel made her a popular writer, she remained in motion. She visited Korea, Siberia, France, and England; when the Sino-Japanese war began she was the first "woman writer" to visit Nanjing after it fell, and wrote about her experiences traveling with the Japanese army to Hankou in works like *Battlefront* (*Sensen*, 1938) and *North Shore Corps* (*Hokugan butai*, 1939). After that, the military sent her south, where she observed places like Singapore, the Malay Peninsula, and Borneo, which became important settings in her later works. Her final work, *Floating Clouds*, was also the story of a vagabond woman.[5] In both *Diary of a Vagabond* and *Floating Clouds*, a female protagonist retraces Hayashi's own movements,

adding new layers to the meaning of this motion. Particularly important is the meaning of the first-person protagonist's motion as a woman. For example, in *Diary of a Vagabond*, motion away from "a woman's place" is crucial. Before, during and after the war (and, in truth, the situation probably remains unchanged today), there were two places women were considered to belong, two positions to which they were assigned: the house they were born and raised in, and the house where they assumed the role of wife and mother. The motion in *Diary of a Vagabond*, in which the narrator separates herself from womanhood by leaving these two houses, is ambivalent, going back and forth between freedom and uncertainty, release and poverty. The act of vagabondage itself is clearly gendered, with a tremendous difference in meaning between a woman's motion and a man's. We might also note that motion in *Diary of a Vagabond* is also created on occasions when the narrator, who wanders between multiple men, deviates from heterosexual desire.

5   *Food* (*Meshi*, 1951), though published immediately after Hayashi's death, was actually an unfinished work. It was in the process of serialization in *The Asahi Shimbun* newspaper, and only two-thirds written.

Yuriko Miyamoto, pioneer of proletarian literature, was also in constant motion. By the age of 19, she was auditing classes at Columbia University in New York. She led a life of travel befitting a "woman of culture" raised by wealthy educators, visiting such cities as Paris and London. However, her close relationship with Russian literary translator Yoshiko Yuasa was, to her, surely also a kind of motion with respect to sexuality. Miyamoto left her husband to live with Yuasa, then later entered into a relationship with a man again; in terms of sexuality she was both migrant and returnee. Of course, her trajectory shows repeated meanderings this way and that, and after her relationship with Yuasa ended, she never again entered into a close relationship involving sexual intimacy and

sensuality with a woman. The letters she exchanged with Yuasa are vividly inscribed not only with Miyamoto's unease and uncertainty about becoming a migrant in terms of sexuality, but also with the conflict over loving Miyamoto felt by Yuasa, who identified as a woman who loved women.[6] Yuasa was notorious for moving from one residence to another inside Japan, and during the seven years Miyamoto and Yuasa were together they were constantly on the move. They took the Siberian Railroad via Busan to Moscow and spent three years based in the USSR, during which time they traveled to Warsaw, Vienna, Berlin, Paris, and other places. Accompanying them during their seven years in motion together was a black trunk bearing the initials "Y.Y.C." Ariko Kurosawa, a literary scholar who edited and analyzed the meaning of their correspondence, quotes Yuasa's words "Love is like a bundle two people carry together" and writes that the trunk contained the air of a mysterious dream called "love and friendship." However, a black trunk that that hides its contents from view is is practically a material manifestation of the relationship the two women shared. Though Miyamoto called the fierce emotion she felt toward Yuasa an "impulse," she was not able to completely escape the idea that love, sex, and sensuality arise only between people of the opposite sex, and tried to regulate their relationship as "friendship"; Yuasa, for her part, recognized what she felt for other women as "love" but thought that love between two women was impossible. Their relationship remained opaque as it moved, like the black trunk that accompanied them everywhere. Kurosawa calls the letters exchanged between Miyamoto and Yuasa a superb text in the literature of love, and finds in them variations on a diverse relationship with "multiple intensities, changeable

6   For a superb critical biography focusing on the period from Yuasa's first meeting with Miyamoto to their parting, see Hitomi Sawabe, *Yuriko, Dasvidaniya: Yuasa Yoshiko no seishun* [Yuriko, Dasvidaniya: The youth of Yoshiko Yuasa] (Tokyo: Bungeishunju, 1990).

colors, obscure motion, and freely mobile configurations" (Foucault).[7] And Kurosawa, who saw in this correspondence "one of countless possibilities that exist amid commonplace everyday life," appears in *of girls* as one of the voices that speak about relationships between women. When people who differ in race, age, gender, and sexuality appear in this work and read aloud Hayashi's novel, Miyamoto's writings, and the correspondence between Miyamoto and Yuasa, the accumulation of voices inscribed with their bodies and memories, emotions and intellects, has an irregular resonance. This fragmented and opaque feminist/queer polyphony remains in motion throughout the work and beyond.

7   Ariko Kurosawa (ed.), *Ofuku shokan: Miyamoto Yuriko to Yuasa Yoshiko* [Letters between Yuriko Miyamoto and Yoshiko Yuasa] (Tokyo: Kanrin Shobo, 2008), 6.

Yuka Kanno
is an Associate Professor at the Doshisha University Graduate
School of Global Studies. Her fields of specialization include
queer studies and film and visual culture studies. She is
interested in issues of gender, sexuality, and race in video art,
and her research explores questions around video art and
activism, the generation of community, and other matters in
the context of queer cinema and movie festivals. Her publications include *Queer Cinema Studies* (Koyo Shobo, 2021)
and contributions to edited volumes such as *The Routledge
Handbook of Japanese Cinema* (Routledge, 2021), *The Japanese
Cinema Book* (Bloomsbury Academic, 2020), *Exploring
Queer Studies* (Koyo Shobo, 2020), *Gender and Biopolitics:
New Readings of Postwar Japan* (Rinsen Book, 2019), and
Yuzo Kawashima Is Born Twice (Suiseisha, 2018).

An opaque feminist/queer polyphony

Film still from *Maurits Script*

《マウリッツ・スクリプト》映像スチル

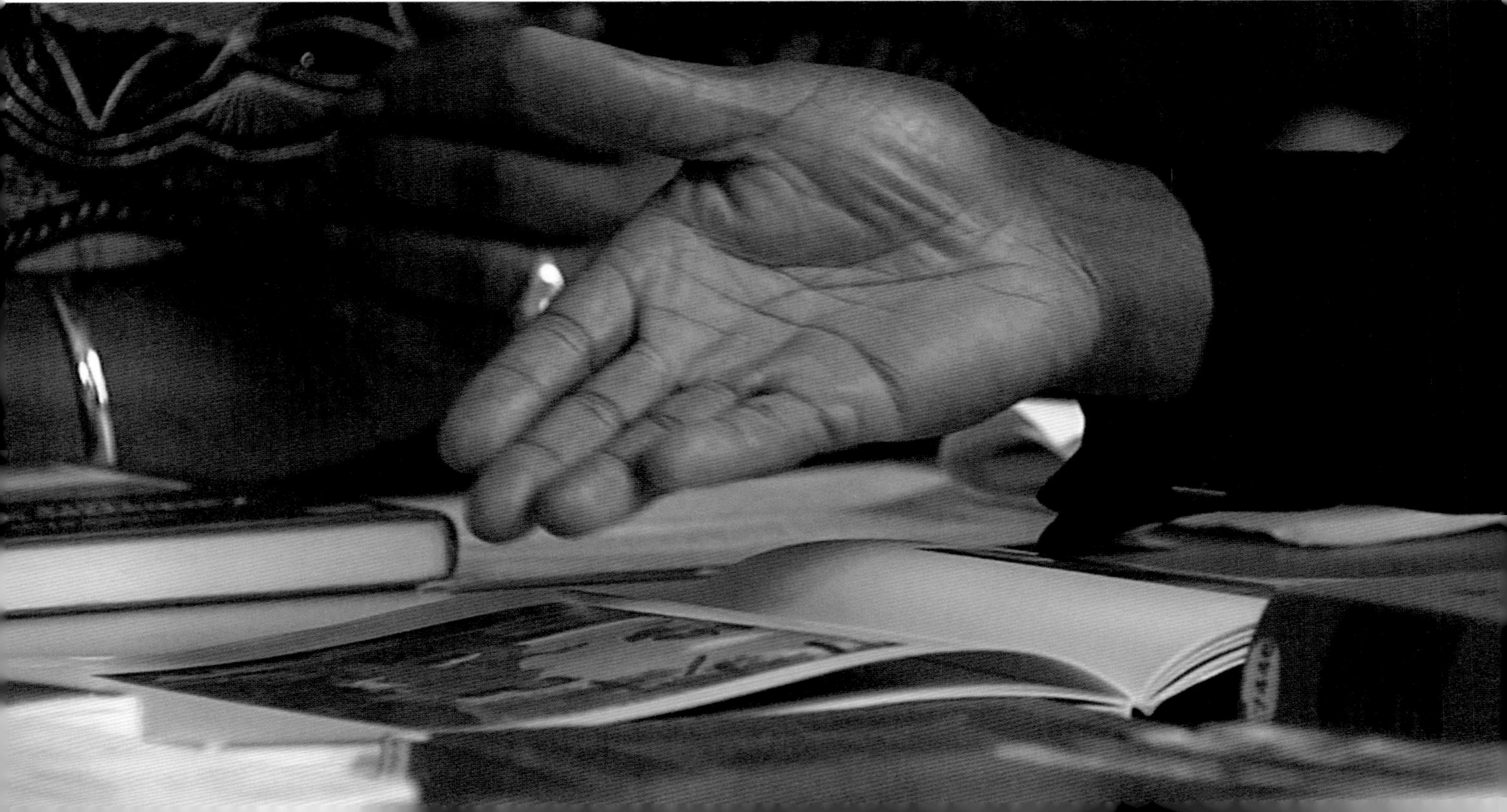

《ふたつの石》映像スチル

Film still from *Two Stones*

Film still from obsada

Film still from *Maurits Script*

《マウリッツ・スクリプト》映像スチル

Film still from *No False Echoes*

《偽りなき響き》映像スチル

Film still from *Hier*.

《ヒア》映像スチル

Film still from *Two Stones*

〈ふたつの石〉映像スチル

〈ふたつの石〉映像スチル

When we assemble

Binna Choi

Lately I had an occasion to visit the Dutch parliament. It was for a hearing on the Netherlands' cultural policy over the coming years. The day-long hearing consisted of several thematic sessions: for each, representatives from the cultural sector gave statements of a few minutes, followed by questions from members of parliament. The whole day was open to the public for observation, but not to pose questions or intervene. (No special instruction was given about this code of behavior but the whole arrangement and procedure somehow made it clear.) Everything ran smoothly in a highly choreographed and moderated manner. All the invited participants were given equally allocated time slots to speak and everyone was well behaved, speaking politely but not modestly, formally but not theatrically. This environment also featured an elaborate support structure, from the high-tech individual microphones to the audio-sensitive interior. It included a man who was serving drinks, as if he was performing, along with what could be his prop, a cabinet with a sliding door filled with glasses, all functioning smoothly while avoiding obstruction to the gathering. And so the speeches continued. This is the space of the so-called democratic institution. In this space different voices are supposed to be heard; exchanges in words take place.

This parliamentary space-time reminded me, somehow, of the space-time in Wendelien van Oldenborgh's films. In many of her works, a group of "actor-participants" gather at a place of particular significance, whether architectural, historical or political. Invited by the artist for their special relation with the content or issue the work addresses, most of these people are vocal in manifesting these relationships in words, coming to a point of discussion, and sometimes argumentation, yet always with respect for each other. The issues of the films are topical, if not provocative, touching on the public discourse particular to a national

or local context while also having wider implications. Also notably, just as everyone speaks in the film, everyone looks elegant as much as eloquent. So too do the "audience-participants" who are present in the films, though they remain as silent witnesses, if not spectators. The diversity tends to work, although the films do not necessarily pursue an immediate consensus. They create a space for listening to, speaking and debating divergent positions and knowledge.

From this experience, I came to ask myself: does it suggest the work of Van Oldenborgh as an exercise of democratic construction? Of course, this comparison between a parliamentary democratic space and the cinematic gathering spaces of Van Oldenborgh will require study and elaboration. It could easily appear reactionary if we simply catalogued how the two forms mirror one another. This would lead to affirming the representative democracy and the assumed harmonious function of communication in its institutional space, which, as we know, is false. Rather, the study should delve into how they actually diverge from each other, and what the differences stand for. It's my intention to launch the beginning of such a study here. In doing so, I take *No False Echoes* (2008) as my focus. The film not only exemplifies characteristics typical of the films that the artist has produced since 2005–in terms of both subject matter and method– but also coincides with the events that shook the "pillars" of the Dutch democratic system, which were followed by an anti-democratic political shift and its corresponding cultural turns.

Bricolage

2008 marks the beginning of the global financial crisis, although this was not yet palpable within the Netherlands. Instead, the discourse around multiculturalism and Islamophobia was dominant, in the aftermath of unprecedented political events that had prompted a rise in nationalism and populist politics. In 2002 Pim Fortuyn, founding leader of the political party LPF (Pim Fortuyn List) was assassinated during the general election. This came at a time when his anti-Muslim and anti-immigration position, delivered in an extremely unapologetic and, if you will, charismatic tone, was rapidly gaining popularity. Just two years later another political assassination was committed: the target was Theo van Gogh, a filmmaker and columnist, who enjoyed provocation and controversy while making blunt critiques of Islamic cultures and multiculturalism. Whilst the murderer in the former case was a white Dutch environmental and animal rights activist (Volkert van der Graaf), Van Gogh's killer was a young Dutch-Morrocan man (Mohammed Bouyeri), which only intensified the uproar on the nationalist —furthermore racist—side. As a response, Dutch cultural policy, in line with the buzzing political and popular analysis on this newly manifest tension and destabilization in Dutch society, turned to focus on multiculturalism. This would have a visible influence on all art and cultural institutional programs, Van Abbemuseum's multifaceted project "Be[com]ing Dutch" being an example. "Be[com] ing Dutch," for which the museum won the Development Prize for Cultural Diversity by the Mondriaan Stichting (now Mondriaan Fonds), consisted not only of an exhibition but also an extensive program of debates, reading groups and nationwide institutional collaborations, unfolding over a two-year period (2007–2008). It is in this context that *No False Echoes* was produced. Commissioned by

the museum, the artist's response was to dive into the recent political events but not to make another provocation or an easy manifestation of a one-sided ideological stance. Instead, she invited multiple voices from various backgrounds and brought our attention to a complex set of interwoven stories; hence, a gathering takes place.

This gathering, however, is not of the representative type. The invited speakers are not, let's say, from the same framework of professional practices and organizations as those who would appear in a parliament (for example, the directors of various cultural institutions speaking for broad parts of the cultural sector at the hearing I attended). And they are not making statements from a designated position, as if in a parliament, representing the entity they come from. Instead, we see a rapper, a radio producer, scholars, an editor—figures who the artist had met through research for the film, but also by contingent encounters —who are here and there, sitting and standing, in and around a building where the gathering takes place. Let us have a closer look:

The one who is standing in the balcony of a building for most of time is the popular Dutch-Moroccan rapper Salah Edin. Just before this appearance, his picture was used in a film by Geert Wilders, another controversial politician with an anti-Islam and anti-immigration stance, but with Edin mistakenly identified as Mohammed Bouyeri, revealing how a racist gaze works.[1] Edin's lyrics are characterized by sociopolitical critique, in particular over the Islamophobic Dutch society as expressed in the song "Het Land Van..." (This Country Of...). In the film, Edin, instead of rapping by his own lyrics, reads "Als ik eens Nederlander was" (If I were a Dutchman), the 1913 text by

1   The picture on the cover of his album *Nederlands Grootste Nachtmerrie* [The Netherlands' Worst Nightmare] features the musician in a way that is similar in appearance to Bouyeri, mocking this gaze.

Indonesian nationalist Soewardi Soerjaningrat, which eloquently criticizes the Dutch colonial authority and strongly evokes the need for Indonesian independence and freedom. With Edin trying to perform the text as much as he can, the film also shows us moments of rehearsal and mistakes. Edin is there as himself, or acting himself, while attempting to embody this historical figure Soerjaningrat who in a different time took an antagonistic position against the Dutch regime. Meanwhile, all the rest of the people sit or stand closely together on a high mezzanine inside the building. The radio producer Wim Noordhoek talks about one of his radio programs, *De Avonden*, where for the period 2002–2004 he broadcasted selections from an archive of Dutch Indonesian colonial-era radio transmissions. Programmed and technologically enabled by the Dutch company Philips since the 1920s, these historical broadcasts addressed both the Dutch population in Indonesia (the former Dutch East Indies) and wealthy Indonesians. As Noordhoek, together with Edwin Jurriëns, a scholar in Indonesian Studies and author of *From Monologue to Dialogue: Radio and Reform in Indonesia* (2009), let us know, it served the process of modernization, bringing European lifestyles closer, and strictly excluded any political propaganda from its broadcasts, focusing on "light" content such as dance music, advice on emotional complex and entertainment. In the pre-television, pre-YouTube era, the radio seems to have acted as the dominant media of the colonial landscape. Yet Baukje Prins, a feminist philosopher and scholar in cultural diversity, brings to light another side of this history. In the Netherlands of the 1920s, the country of the colonizers, different ideological and religious communities settled into an agreement for coexistence—so-called "sectarianism" or "pillarization"—through remaining separate from each other in order to reduce conflict and the need to negotiate. This was at the cost of secular, liberal and humanist Dutch

communities making concessions to anti-revolutionary and conservative parties.

Can a gathering like the one found in *No False Echoes* be best characterized as a form of democratic pluralism? If so, then perhaps this is one that does not exist in reality yet? The notion of bricolage, as Homi K. Bhabha introduces, might give one articulation:

> [Bricolage] allows you to relate to a tradition or various traditions of thinking and yet to articulate something different, or something original, or something distinctive, without participating in the kind of temporal and conceptual irresponsibility which suggests that something is old and something is new.[2]

2   Interview with Homi K. Bhabha by Solange de Boer and Zoe Gray, in *Source Book 1: Brian Jungen* (Rotterdam: Witte de With, 2006), 24.

Bhabha further elaborates that bricolage does not have a totality or a boundary. It refers to the uncertain ground on which we stand, turning an issue towards particular, temporary instances allowing unconventional trajectories and movements of thinking, rather than reducing them to homogeneous or separable matters. When Bhabha goes on say that the bricoleur "feels that the haunting of the past, the ghosts of the past are never put outside the door," I feel convinced that it's bricolage that is taking place in Van Oldenborgh's films, and that Van Oldenborgh is a bricoleur.

The artist—the invisible presider of this gathering— bricolages fragments from the unresolved past of anti-colonial struggles/independence movements as well as the societal change during the same era in the Netherlands, along with the history of technological development and the media landscape, exploring their entanglement with

the transition that Dutch society, and the West in general, has been undergoing since the turn of the [20th] century in relation to its "others." Bhabha says that the practices of bricolage "allow you to *hang on to that temporality of transition.*"[3] Not knowing what's going to happen, you are committed to the contingent paths of transition as a stepping stone. The bricolage-gathering might be a pertinent form for our times—a means of transition towards the unknown, in democracy as well as art. It indicates there is more work to do now and that we might be part of it, along with all the baggage of past and future.

3   Bhabha interview, 24, [emphasis mine].

Study Group

Those who gather in the film all read: reading their own texts as well as those written by others both present and past. This differs from the reading of a script by memorizing it. Often the texts are visible in the film, and the act of reading is not masked by the performance. Rather, the speakers move between inactive forms of reading, performing the text, and speaking by themselves; blurring what the performance is and is not, what one's opinion is and is not, what part of the story is from the past and what is from the present. What does this situation of ambiguity intend to create? How does the reading of these fragments, loaded with historical and contemporary political/societal information, enable us, those who remain silent, to read? What kind of consensus or political process could be made from this? A study group, is my response.

Study may, for some, have a secondary status to the notion of research. Study is what you do with the guidance of someone, with an absence of autonomy. But study is, as

Fred Moten and Stefano Harney put forward, a speculative practice that is already happening among those who struggle in common in a situation like "being in a kind of workshop, playing in a band, in a jam session, or old men sitting on a porch, or people working together in a factory," just not in a classroom or lecture hall.[4] Research today is being co-opted for corporate interests and controlled by the managerial class, as seen in a number of universities—yet ironically, teachers and students alike still see themselves as distinct from workers. Moten and Harney argue that study is instead a "common intellectual practice," of workers, so-called intellectuals and in fact anyone—in as much as they are in relation with one another in opposition to something that dominates and oppresses such forms of study for the sake of institutionalization, capitalization and colonization.

4   See "Studying through the Undercommons: Stefano Harney and Fred Moten Interviewed by Stevphen Shukaitis," November 12, 2012, *Class War University*, http://class waru.org/2012/11/12/studying-through-the-undercommons-stefano-harney-fred-moten-interviewed-by-stevphen-shukaitis/.

A bricolage-work of positions, thoughts and ideas across different times and cultures taking place in *No False Echoes* might well be considered a situation of study.[5] Each reading is responsive to another, leading to a conversation and speculative futuring. It invites the viewers into a mode of study, too. The speakers and the audiences (inside and outside the films) alike are called for study, deliberating on what has happened to the seemingly peaceful and democratic Dutch society, how what is forgotten or unthought casts light on the current state of things—or what

5   Although it is not a focus in this essay, it would be meaningful to think of this notion of study as taking place in and further exemplified by another work by the artist: *Instruction* (2009). This film takes place at the Netherlands Defense Academy with young cadets as the protagonists, reading texts and discussing the Dutch military intervention in Indonesia against the Indonesian independence efforts of the late 1940s. The cadets deliberate on—study together—the scope of ethics of their conduct in such a situation, where the instruction or command is a rule but ethical and political indiscernibility reigns.

When we assemble

we could learn from those past-fragments, how media
and "new" technology produce effects/affects within
the societal and political climate and so on. If the Dutch
democratic system had found another route for dealing
with dissent and conflict instead of pillarization, might
it have avoided the current confrontational situation,
in which society is divided into Islamophobes, immigrants,
et cetera? Baukje Prins seems to think so, and explains
this in terms of feminist modes of thinking and practices
of "intersectionalism." Or does the current sensitivity
about media "freedom of speech" resemble the monopoly
of the media under the Suharto dictatorship in Indonesia?
Edwin Jurriëns's story on the latter might insinuate so,
yet it is complexified by other voices. Who controls, runs
and pays today's media? What's the influence of popular
culture such as hip-hop? And so on and so on. Endless
bricolage comes with endless study.

In their conception of study, Moten and Harney also rely
on the experience of jazz improvisation, which also contrasts
itself from the modes of planning and logistics that are
emblematic of capitalist behavior. This improvisation
corresponds with the notion of polyphony, one of the crucial
concepts in Van Oldenborgh's practice. This does not simply
require a multiplicity of voices, but also their intersection
or tuning to another, becoming looser in each one's
boundary and forming collective rhythms. Here we could
look to Terry Eagleton to affirm improvisation as an alternative mode of political work. While asserting the aim of
politics is to secure the "good life," Eagleton argues this
good life can be envisioned through the working process
of an improvised jazz group:

> A jazz group which is improvising obviously
> differs from a symphony orchestra, since to a large
> extent each member is free to express herself as

she likes. But she does so with a receptive sensitivity to the self-expressive performances of the other musicians. The complex harmony they fashion comes not from playing from a collective score, but from the free musical expression of each member acting as the basis for the free expression of the others. As each player grows more musically eloquent, the others draw inspiration from this and are spurred to greater heights.[6]

6   Terry Eagleton, *The Meaning of Life* (Oxford: Oxford University Press, 2007), 174.

7   Wendelien van Oldenborgh, unpublished interview with KUNCI Cultural Studies Center, 2008.

Van Oldenborgh has expressed that the gatherings she presides in often amaze her, in terms of how people are willing to engage and offer their thoughts and experiences. And, next to this amazement, she adds that "the way they see or place themselves within the process of the work varies I think, but it always *is* a negotiation."[7] A mode of study lies in the improvisational practice. There's no totality that rules but each own in tune with one another. Isn't this the foundation for "democracy"?

Punctum

The building where *No False Echoes* was shot, where the gathering took place, is Radio Kootwijk, which was built as a transmission station around 1920, when radio contact was first established between Holland and the Dutch East Indies. As an early modernist building it has a Brutalist magnificence and roughness, exuding the power of its presence. Yet emptied of all the machines that enabled the voice of the "motherland" to reach the colony—machines that apparently became obsolete soon after their installation—its ghostly vacuousness resonates with much of what cannot be spoken. A shot of Edin reading "Als ik

een Nederlander was" from a balcony shows a glimpse of the surrounding barren landscape. Whenever the film pauses—the moments when the performativity is interrupted with the low tone of rehearsal, conversation, or laughter—the facade of the building confronts us.

The sight is accompanied by sounds from the landscape such as birds singing, but it is also followed by a lullaby, one that is popular both in the Netherlands and in Indonesia and sung in Indonesian in both countries. Functionally, this indicates a moment of transition to the indoor gathering. This gathering so full of verbal exchanges is intercepted with varied pauses, intervals, and deviations (from words to images). It's like how radio at the turn of the last century in Indonesia worked, according Rudolf Mrázek.[8] Around the late 19th century, life in the Dutch East Indies was crowded with telegraph, telephone, and postal communication, which, as Mrázek suggests, exuded a sense of nearness, proximity, and connectivity between different places. But, he argues, with the arrival of direct wireless communication—namely radio—the euphoria was gone. For the Dutch, depression and nostalgia were mounting in anticipation of the country's capitulation to the Japanese during World War II and the loss of its colony; Indonesians were feeling rising discontent resulting from the discriminatory rule of the colonial regime. The radio, for Mrázek, was a transitory apparatus signaling political and cultural shifts at a time when no one quite knew what was going to happen, ironically amplifying a vacuum or silence in contrast to what sounded like never-ending talks and music.

8   Rudolf Mrázek, *Engineers of Happy Land: Technology and Nationalism in a Colony* (Princeton, NJ: Princeton University Press, 2002).

Here it becomes clear that the situation of study group or bricolage cannot be defined by verbal exchange alone.

The conversation and the negotiation taking place within it have another, unspoken undertone. I would like to name it by borrowing the notion of "punctum" from Roland Barthes's *Camera Lucida* (*La Chambre claire,* 1980). In his semiotic (or, rather, anti-semiotic) account of the nature of the photographic image, Barthes contrasts the punctum with the notion of *studium*—the Latin origin of the word "study"—that is defined by societal, political, and cultural codes. Punctum, resistant to *studium*, is an accidental feature or quality, one that the author of the image cannot intend, but that comes anyway. It is associated with pain—a sting or pinch—embodying time or "that-has-been."[9]

9   "This new *punctum*, which is no longer of form but of intensity, is Time, the lacerating emphasis of the noeme ('*that-has-been*'), its pure representation." Roland Barthes, *Camera Lucida* (New York: Hill & Wang, 1981), 96.

This may be understood as the experience of the subjective relation between a viewer and a photographed subject. Or this is what makes "study" genuine. Harney and Moten's notion of study can be only substantiated with the notion of "Black." When they refer to study, they mean Black study. Black study as collective resistance is built upon the long history of painful but persistent struggles of Black communities against enclosures, slavery, and racism. We un/learn to study from their pain-ridden yet fugitive, resilient, and liberating struggles.

The building facade as captured in the film comes as a punctum, something that the architect of that progressive time could not have anticipated. The accompanying bird-song no one can fail to understand, but could have been recorded anywhere, at any time, and is an acoustic punctum. The lullaby is everyone's punctum, yet with a singular, particular memory of each listener or singer —that which once one had but now has lost—analogous to the experience of separation from one's mother by

being born, and later, inevitably, by a shared mortality.[10] The kind of study and bricolage that makes the assembly, as in *No False Echoes* or as in our desiring forms of democracy, is enacted upon the encountering and acknowledgment of the punctum.

10   As a private but meaningful note, it was the artist's daughter who sang the lullaby. The artist also has a personal relationship with the Dutch colonial past in Indonesia in that this was where her grandparents and mother lived.

Does today's democracy know the punctum? Unfortunately not—certainly not in its institutional space. Squares and roundabouts around the world might be filled with those shedding and quickly wiping tears as they cry for solidarity, but the parliamentary space-time has lost all the music, all the bricolage, and the punctum. *No False Echoes* is a reminder of what other kinds of space-time and gathering may be possible—so long as we don't forget to study and improvise in our hidden tears.

Written October 2015, revised October 2022

Binna Choi

is a curator, and the director at Casco Art Institute: Working
for the Commons, Utrecht in the Netherlands, exploring the
commons as an alternative to binary worldviews and systems
through and for art. The key projects include Grand Domestic
Revolution (2009-2012 with Maiko Tanaka), Site for Unlearning
(Art Organization) (2014-2018 with Annette Krauss and
the Casco team), Travelling Farm Museum of Forgotten Skills
(2018- ongoing with the Outsiders). For the Singapore Biennale
2022: *Natasha*, Choi is co-artistic director and previously
served as the curator for Gwangju Biennale 2016: *The Eighth
Climate (What Does Art Do)*. Choi is a member of the Academy
of the Arts of the World, Cologne, Germany, an advisor for Afield
international network, and the co-initiators of Electric Palm
Tree with Kyongfa Che and Unmapping Eurasia with Mi You.

When we assemble

Film still from of girls

《彼女たちの》映像スチル

《オブサダ》映像スチル

Film still from *obsada*

Film still from *Hier*.

《ヒア》撮影記録 撮影：ヤコブ・ダニレヴィッチ

Production still from *Hier.*, photo by Jakub Danilewicz

Production still from *Maurits Script*, photo by Nienke Terpsma

《マウリッツ・スクリプト》撮影記録　撮影：ニンケ・テルプスマ

Production still from *of girls*

《彼女たちの》撮影記録

《オブサダ》映像スチル

Film still from *obsada*

《偽りなき響き》映像スチル

Film still from *No False Echoes*

An image of study

Pablo de Ocampo

The filmmaker Peter Watkins is perhaps best known for his 1966 film *The War Game*, a mock-documentary about a British city in the aftermath of a nuclear attack. The film was initially intended for BBC broadcast, but the BBC decided it was too shocking for general television audiences. In utilizing the format and language of a documentary, with broadcast-news-style reportage and interviews, Watkins's film has a tone disturbingly close to the language of reality. As a narrative, it resonated with the circumstances and context of the time: the 1960s was very much the peak of the Cold War and the looming threat of nuclear war was quite real, perhaps most critically in the standoff between the Soviet Union and the United States in Cuba early in that decade.

Two decades later, Watkins followed this work with *The Journey* (1987), a film less widely seen, though certainly notorious for its scale: produced over several years, ranging across more than a dozen countries, and clocking in at more than 14 hours. Like *The War Game*, *The Journey* is rooted in the Cold War and the proliferation of nuclear weapons from the end of World War II through the 1980s. Yet while sharing a sociopolitical context and the broad goals of critiquing the military-industrial complex and working toward nuclear abolition, the two films offer different strategies and approaches.

To generalize, documentary or nonfiction film strives to teach or convey some truth to viewers. For example, *The War Game* served to proliferate a more comprehensive understanding of the threat of nuclear war, issuing a warning siren about nuclear armaments through the speculative imagining of a bomb blast. While *The Journey* served similar end purposes in its anti-nuclear messaging, it was built around process as much as final product.

The Journey's outcome was entirely entangled with shared learning and an engaged production process. The individuals on screen are neither characters nor subjects but active agents in dialogue with the filmmakers. Spanning 15 different countries, they bring their own expertise, but not from positions of definitive authority. The participants, directly and indirectly, touched by the effects of the nuclear arms race, share experiences and ask questions of one another and the filmmaker. Watkins's work on *The Journey* served not just an end goal of conveying information to an audience; it instigated a collaborative exchange of learning among all the stakeholders in its production.

I've been thinking about *The Journey* in relation to the films of Wendelien van Oldenborgh in terms of their shared investment in collaborative models of production. Like Watkins, Van Oldenborgh works in a documentary mode, reflecting or representing "the real," but ultimately, her work is more nuanced. The unique strengths of Van Oldenborgh's films reside in their production of an image of study. They demonstrate that creating an image of study is not a question of framing and composition—what an image *is*—but rather of process—*how* an image is made.

In *Maurits Script* (2006), the earliest work on view in Van Oldenborgh's exhibition *unset on-set*, a series of quick cuts introduces us to the film's characters, framed up close against a backdrop of the gilded walls of the Mauritshuis museum in the Hague (the museum was in fact once the home of Johan Maurits van Nassau). The characters are all key figures from the Dutch colonial period in Brazil in the mid-17th century. As the titles scroll by, we see that each is represented by multiple participants in the film.

One of them opens a book on a table and begins to leaf through it. At first, the book shown reflects the character

of the museum's interior: finely bound and weighty with power and history. But as the pages turn, we see that the volume is interleaved with loose A4 printed sheets of paper. The official tome, we realize, has been annotated, complicated, amended. The woman begins to read aloud narrative fragments chronicling the experiences of Johan Maurits van Nassau while he served as governor of the Dutch colonial territory in Brazil.

As this unfolds, different participants cycle in, speaking from multiple perspectives around this history. These individuals are neither performing nor reciting texts but actively reading aloud. It's a subtle distinction, but an essential gesture in this production of an image of study. What's more, we see all these participants in the museum's public space. Though the framing of the shots is often tight to a single person, we catch glimpses of the production crew and museum visitors passing by as the study sessions transpire. These images signal an important distinction: this is public study, thinking out loud. Though the Dutch colonial period in Brazil was brief, it becomes clear through these texts that this brutal period was not inconsequential. The participants come from differing backgrounds, grappling with details of events from hundreds of years before and relating to them through the lens of the lasting impacts of this history on contemporary Dutch society.

Maurits Script contains many elements upon which Van Oldenborgh's films are built. There is an architecture, a text, and a group of participants. These elements are all unique to each of her films, and they always operate together, interconnectedly. This is to say, her films are not so much about books, buildings, or individuals, but use these components in combination to frame a structure, pose a question, and engender a coming together of individuals in the shared pursuit of study.

These are textual films, but not in the sense that they emanate from a script, in a traditional theatrical or dramaturgical model; there is no "story" that is being adapted for actors. Rather, texts form the basis for the work by providing a point from which to launch an inquiry, and a pedagogical model. The texts don't proclaim or demonstrate truths but facilitate engagement with the margins of official histories, charting personal relationships and resonances across boundaries of time and cultural understanding.

Though many of the films have characters or subjects, these are often historical figures cited and sometimes quoted, not the people we see on the screen. The individuals who appear in the films are better categorized as participants, given how their presence is not simply about speaking lines but about being active collaborators. The participants appear as themselves, both to tell their stories and to engage in a process of inquiry. As contemporary subjects, the collaborators are shown reading, conversing with one another, and questioning the histories and places in which they live.

Just as the participants are more than just characters, the places they appear in are more than mere sets or backdrops. The architectures, like the people, are full of resonances and relationships. Van Oldenborgh's process probes how architectures can reflect histories. She uses the spaces to stage dialogues between the people who designed and built them, their historical functions, and the people who inhabit them in the present. *Maurits Script* is sited at the Mauritshuis museum, a place key to the history it investigates. Another early film, *No False Echoes* (2008), takes place at Radio Kootwijk, the transmission site from which the first radio contact was established to the Dutch colonies in Indonesia.

As in *Maurits Script*, a book marks the start of *Two Stones*
(2019). The film opens in the courtyard of a housing
complex. A medium shot shows a woman seated on a bench
reading from a book on her lap: "With each document,
a sensation of false surprise is renewed within me.
The already well-known realization that the language of
the past does not remain fixed in yesteryear, but rather
is regurgitated all too readily in the present." This frames
a narrative situated in the space between two figures,
between two places, and across multiple temporalities,
from "yesteryear" through to the "present."

The film charts a path between two women—the architect
Lotte Stam-Beese and the Caribbean activist and writer
Hermina Huiswoud—both of whom worked in the Soviet
Union in the 1930s and lived in the Netherlands after
the war. As the participants speak, a picture emerges of
these women and the film's locations. Stam-Beese designed
both of the housing complexes in the film: one in Kharkiv,
Ukraine, in the 1930s and the other in Rotterdam,
the Netherlands, in the 1950s. She was one of the first
women trained in architecture at the Bauhaus, and she
designed this housing with a kind of utopian vision for
how communities might live together. The film's participants, all women, move through the housing complexes'
spaces, reflecting on how the structures served the people
living there. Huiswoud's perspective from the 1970s
counters the positive reflections and impacts with her
critiques of Rotterdam housing policies, which restricted
the percentage of Caribbean Dutch in each city district
and adversely impacted the idealistic community Stam-
Beese envisioned.

These multiple narratives and points of view are brought
together in the film's form. It is a single-channel film,
and at about 30 minutes in, the images begin to repeat.

Yet while the image sequence progresses in the same order as in the film's first half, the soundtrack diverges, with a different sound edit overlaid on this second run-through. On repeat viewing, the sound design makes itself more apparent. Though the film is full of people on screen whose voices we hear, the sound is not actually synchronous with the images. This asynchronous edit allows Van Oldenborgh to weave a whole new conversation into the film, where characters in repeated scenes express different sentiments. This structure extends the conversations and references in the narrative, with each part circling back to the other, participants being in conversation with themselves through time.

In one such scene, the first audio track discusses the limits of change and progress, with the participant Hannah Dawn Henderson offering the frustrated observation that "you don't resolve the history of sexism and oppression of women by simply removing the kitchen." When the scene comes back around the second time, Henderson speaks of her history as a racialized individual and how she ultimately transcends some of the powerlessness she has felt with hope.

Hier. (2021) opens in a vaulted room at the Museum Arnhem. We watch a group of young women, who make up the band FRED, playing guitar, bass, and ukulele. As the band fills the space with a spare melody of the genre kroncong, two other participants' voices are heard. One speaks to this Indo-European form, calling it at one point a kind of "melancholic colonial song." As the band plays on, these two participants, Lara Nuberg and Pelumi Adejumo, walk through different parts of the museum, interjecting in between songs by the band. They outline the history of kroncong, characterizing it as a product of European colonialism and speaking to the music's cultural

An image of study

relevance and nostalgic qualities for Indo-Europeans living in the Netherlands.

Though both Nuberg and Adejumo are writers, the text in the film, the foundational component through which dialogue and inquiry develop, is the music. Music sets off personal reflections and reactions. Nuberg, who is of Indo-European descent, relates the songs to her mother and grandmother—to her family's lineage back before they came to the Netherlands. She speaks of a certain in-betweenness that her family found themselves in as former colonial subjects, coming from the Dutch East Indies yet not having a connection to modern Indonesia. For Adejumo, a poet originally from Nigeria, her personal reflections begin with other points of musical interest, from Billie Eilish to Freddie Mercury. As Adejumo listens, kroncong sparks musings about home and memory. Surrounded by the sounds in the hall, she writes: "Can you dream of music you've never heard before? Just like a land where you were born but never found a route of return?"

Like the song tradition being performed, these women all speak from positions of hybridity, diaspora, identity, and cultural belonging. The music provides one frame through which to consider their lives, and the building opens another. The Museum Arnhem was built in the 19th century and originally functioned as a social club for men of lower social standing, which generally meant those from the "colonies." In the film, it is in the middle of a massive renovation: its walls are stripped down to the bones, scaffolding supports the structure, and rough concrete cuts through where doors once were. It's a building with a colonial past that is in the process of transformation, of becoming something else.

The band punctuates all these moments with bits of song. In one shot, the camera looks from above as a hand places the needle on a spinning 78 rpm record. The scratchy sound that emanates is a historical example of kroncong, and after a few bars of the record playing, FRED begins to play along and riff away in their own direction. It's not until the film's final few minutes that the band plays an uninterrupted full performance. Up until this point they've been listening, rehearsing, studying the form of kroncong. All that we hear them play back throughout the film is reformulated here as their own original song, infused with elements from this musical lineage.

obsada (2021) opens with the sound of steady, deep breathing. The camera looks down at a chair on a wood floor, and two off-screen voices say:

"I'm focusing."

"Me too."

It's a playful double meaning, referencing at first the measured breath of the one participant and then, as the scene unfolds, the action of a second, who is operating the focus of a camera off-screen. The film takes place in two locations in Łódź: Muzeum Sztuki and the Film School. Making visible the mechanism of production is something present across Van Oldenborgh's work—cameras come into frame, boom mics are visible—although here, the production process and crew members are the subjects of the film itself. Gathered together in the two locations is a group of women who serve as the participants—both on-screen, in dialogue and conversation with one another, and also serving as the crew responsible for the production in

collaboration with Van Oldenborgh. The women speak freely about the experiences that brought them to this work, for instance their studies at university, their parents and family, choices they've made in their professional lives, and the different roles they've worked in film production. A recurring theme is how gender biases have affected them. They speak of being taken advantage of, boundaries not being respected, being yelled at by domineering male colleagues, and the need to continue to tolerate all this to keep progressing in their work.

Their conversations are broken up by sequences of choreographed poses and camera framing experiments with sheets of transparent colored acrylic held in front of the lens. These elements point back to a specific history originating at the Łódź Film School through the Workshop of the Film Form, a movement that was organized around the practice of radically rethinking the form and structure of cinema. Alongside its formal experiments, the Workshop often undertook collaborative models of production in an attempt to mirror radical form in their process. But the ideals that drove it were not without their blind spots. Although there were some women, it was a heavily male-dominated space. Like many avant-garde movements, women were largely left out and forgotten.

As the women study photographs of the Workshop's history, they begin to re-create some of the projects from that time period, including one staged at Muzeum Sztuki in 1973. Cameras focus on reflections or film through transparent surfaces; the film frame is bifurcated, layered, and otherwise obscured. Where Workshop projects from the 1970s did include women, they were sometimes, as is the case in the 1971 film *Open Form – Game on an Actress' Face*, literally just surfaces upon which the filmmakers could experiment. Now, the women reimagine this history and collectively insert themselves into it.

Earlier in *obsada* we see the women watching a video projection of Helke Sander's 1978 film *The All-Around Reduced Personality - ReduPers*, whose narrative features a single mother and photographer (played by Sander) who can't make ends meet. Though working in Berlin, Sander was a contemporary of the Workshop in Łódź, and her placement here by Van Oldenborgh shines a light on historical examples of women experimenting with film form. And, of course, this gesture is not simply for the audience, as *obsada*'s participants are studying this in the process of their work. It's worth noting that Van Oldenborgh's citation of *The All-Around Reduced Personality - ReduPers* echoes that film, since Sander likewise cited films by women such as Yvonne Rainer or Valie Export in her work.

Women have always featured prominently as participants in Van Oldenborgh's projects, but in this trio of recent films, the participants directly frame their participation around gender. Early in *Two Stones*, Huiswoud's writing in the journal *Negro Worker* is referenced concerning her perspective at the intersection of class struggle, racism, and sexism—essentially, what it means to be a working-class woman of color. It's a statement that provides the participants a frame through which to consider their place in relation to the different articulations of feminist ideas by Huiswoud and Stam-Beese. In *Hier.*, where the participants gather in the halls of the museum under renovation, there is a palpable sense of how their very presence is actively redefining the building's structures of authority, legacy, and representation. The women in *obsada*, in reflecting on their shared experiences of sexism in the film industry, end with a discussion on whether the changes they hope to see in their field are even possible:

An image of study

"So the question is whether we, as the bridge between the old world and the new one, have already lost, or can we still ... I don't know."

"I believe we can. But sometimes I'm naive."

"Do we have to die out for things to change?"

The film ends without conclusions or answers. But the films of Van Oldenborgh are never finite. The participants she works with are shown gaining agency in a continually generative process. "Change has to begin with somebody. It could be us."

Pablo de Ocampo
is director and curator of Moving Image at the Walker Art
Center in Minneapolis, Minnesota. From 2014 to 2020, de
Ocampo held the position of exhibitions curator at the artist-
run center Western Front in Vancouver, Canada. His previous
positions include artistic director of Toronto's Images Festival
from 2006 to 2014, co-founder/collective member of Cinema
Project in Portland, Oregon, and in 2013, programmer of
the 59th Robert Flaherty Film Seminar, *History is What's
Happening.* His writing has appeared in *Canadian Art,
C Magazine, BlackFlash,* and in the catalogues *Dissident Lines:
Lis Rhodes* (Nottingham Contemporary, 2019), and *Low Relief:
Lucy Raven* (EMPAC, Mousse, and Portikus, 2018).

An image of study

《ヒア》撮影記録 撮影：ヤコプ・ダニレヴィッチ

Production still from *Hier.*, photo by Jakub Danilewicz

《彼女たちの》撮影記録

Production still from of girls

《マウリッツ・スクリプト》映像スチル

Film still from *Maurits Script*

Production still from *obsada*, photo by Jakub Danilewicz

《オブサダ》撮影記録　撮影：ヤコブ・ダニレヴィッチ

Production still from *No False Echoes*, photo by Sirtjo Koolhof

《偽りなき響き》撮影記録　撮影：セルチォ・コルホフ

Film still from *Two Stones*

《ふたつの石》映像スチル

《ふたつの石》映像スチル

Film still from *Two Stones*

Film still from *obsada* 《オブサダ》映像スチル

Wendelien van Oldenborgh: An interview

Andrew Maerkle

Tokyo, September 14, 2022

Andrew Maerkle (AM): As I was reviewing your practice in preparation for this interview, I found myself tracing some triangular topoi that recur in your works. One triangle looks at the links between the Netherlands, Indonesia, and Brazil or South America, loosely mapping out the contours of Dutch colonialism. Another triangle looks at the intersections of film, architecture, and music. What keeps you returning to these themes?

Wendelien van Oldenborgh (WvO): The geography is somewhat biographical. My mother was born in Indonesia, so my own family history leads me there. The Dutch were in Indonesia for 300 years, and following decolonization in 1949 some 300,000 Indo-European and Dutch families were repatriated to the Netherlands. We see their influence in everything from food to music genres, such as Indo rock, which was hugely popular in the 1950s. In the case of Brazil, I am personally connected to the country via family ties—I've spent a lot of family time there over the past 20 years—but then it turns out that Brazil was also a Dutch colony at one point.

Obviously I don't want the work to be reduced to biography, but I think artists make the strongest work when they come from a deep understanding, which starts from personal experience. You can use the emotional understanding that you build up though life while adding to it through intellect. And of course not all of my works are about the legacy of Dutch colonialism, but there was a period starting in 2005 or 2006 when I realized that not so many artists at the time were looking at that history and how it connected to contemporary issues in the Netherlands, from housing to patriarchy. *No False Echoes* (2008) is one of the works that resulted from that research.

AM: How about your use of film, architecture, and music?

WvO: Cinema was always an icon for me because it's a multifarious medium that accommodates many layers and forms of affect. But initially it just didn't feel open to me as a practice. Then at a certain point I realized that I could use film-making methods to make anything. I approached it as an experiment: How can I make something by pretending it's a film production?

After some experimentation, *Maurits Script* (2006) was the first project I made as a moving image work. In this case, I started out with a script but was following the regular steps of making a film only in concept. I wanted to open up a method for creating something that is not solely my voice or knowledge but allows other people's voices and knowledges to enter too.

I also had to teach myself editing to be able to assemble all those voices and perspectives into something readable for an audience. I discovered that I really like editing. I think it has a lot to do with music—I also DJ sometimes. Editing is structural and rhythmic. First you have to take a meta position and think very structurally and then you have to let the rhythm take you, otherwise it doesn't work.

AM: Does that feed into your use of music?
WvO: Music brings another insight into the work. It's not a discourse, it's not an image. It provides its own special combination of affect and emotion and information. But I only include music in the work if there's a reason for people to do it in the shoot. I never add it in as a soundtrack.

AM: So your use of kroncong music in works like *No False Echoes* and *Hier.* (2021) is meant to communicate the complex realities of contemporary Dutch society?
WvO: Yes. Kroncong originates in Indonesia with the Portuguese contact in the 16th century. Its modern

iteration, which typically incorporates backing from a ukulele-like string instrument, was popularized in the 19th century by Indo-European theater groups who started to make songs in Malay, which was the lingua franca of the archipelago. In that sense kroncong was emancipatory because it enabled people who felt caught between the local populace and the Dutch colonizers to express themselves in their own voice. It became incredibly popular, aided by the introduction of the gramophone and record companies' strategic cultivation of popular markets all over the world, even though it was never accepted as high culture. But kroncong has a melancholic sound to begin with, and after decolonization and repatriation it became a nostalgic music for Dutch people and those of Indo-European descent to remember the colonial era.

    No False Echoes was specifically looking at colonial Dutch policies controlling the use of radio in the Dutch East Indies. My daughter, who was eight years old at the time, is the one who sings "Nina Bobo" in the film, but the surprising thing is that she had actually learned the song at school. For *Hier.* I asked the members of the all-girl band FRED, who come from a range of backgrounds, including Indonesia, Suriname, and the Netherlands, to analyze kroncong music and see what they could make of it from a contemporary perspective. Then I asked another of the protagonists, Lara, who has an Indo-European background, to talk about the history of the music in connection with her family, which traces back four generations to Indonesia. As suggested by the title *Hier.*, I wanted to focus on how young people express their contemporaneity and agency today, but I would even call it a sentimental work. It stirs those sentiments that music and cinema are especially adept at stirring.

        AM: You take an opposite tack with *Two Stones* (2019), in which two large housing projects,

KhTZ in Kharkiv, Ukraine, which dates to
the Soviet era in the 1930s, and Pendrecht in
Rotterdam, the Netherlands, which was built
in the postwar era of the 1950s, are as much
protagonists as the two historical figures you
deal with in the film, the German architect
Lotte Stam-Beese and the Afro-Caribbean
activist Hermina Huiswoud. In this work you
play the visuals, the audio, and the subtitles
against each other to pull the viewer's attention
in different directions. There's a Brechtian
distancing effect going on.

WvO: I think what's important is that viewers get a sense
that Lotte Stam-Beese and Hermina Huiswoud are
simultaneously connected and disconnected. Both Lotte
and Hermina were attracted to socialist ideology because
of its message of equality. But while Lotte was focused on
making equal architecture for everyone, her equality was
limited to only those who are white, whereas Hermina was
campaigning against regulations in 1970s Rotterdam that
excluded the Surinamese-Dutch population from equal
access to housing. There are inconsistencies between the two
even though they share certain core values, just as contemporary discussions of intersectionality have shown us that
white feminism has not always been aligned with struggles
for racial equality in the United States and Europe.

The work attempts to recover some of those
obscured histories. For example, I didn't know much about
Lotte, who was the first female architecture student at
the Bauhaus, until I took an interest in Pendrecht and
wondered how this major postwar urban planning project
had come to be designed by a woman. Lotte was driven
by a vision of equal housing, but now all the units in
Pendrecht have been privatized and are being traded on
the market, which completely goes against the original
intent. You can't just look at these histories as the past.

You can't look at colonialism without also looking at capitalism or patriarchy. All of them are interlinked.

AM: You specifically address issues of gender and feminism in one of your most recent projects, *obsada* (2021), which you filmed with an all-female cast and crew in Poland.

WvO: Let me first state that my works really are objects of study, because I'm always curious about what I can find by listening to others. I don't come with preconceived answers to the questions I set out for myself. In the case of *obsada*, I wanted to know how these younger women imagine themselves working in an industry that is out-wardly still male-dominated. For instance, when I work on a project I always look for female crew members and it's difficult to find them. They're around, but it's not obvious. This time I was working with students and graduates of the Łódź Film School, which is the biggest film school in Poland. There was a huge controversy just before we started filming because a student had spoken out about abuse of power there. It wasn't meant to be addressed in the work, but it comes through in some of the dialogues, like when one participant says she's glad she didn't go to the school because she was able to avoid suffering under that kind of instruction. During filming it was mind-blowing once the women started talking because they had never discussed these issues with each other before—especially with regard to the doubts and insecurities they face as women in the film industry. It completely surpassed my expectations.

AM: It's like the performative elements in your works function as an exorcism. Or, rather, in having people talk or perform in a historic space, you bring the history of that space back to the surface for viewers, and that archaeological act

in turn becomes a kind of exorcism. I felt this all the more strongly in *obsada*, where the space seems to be folded in on itself.

WvO: We filmed at the school set in Łódź. Roman Polanski filmed there during his time at the school, as did Krzysztof Kieślowski. The space was built as a practice set, so students can make scenes in the rooms and paint the walls and do whatever. But what most interested me was that you can stand on top and see that it's a set, which is maybe why the space appears folded to you.

The other location in the film is the Muzeum Sztuki, also in Łódź, where in the 1970s the all-male experimental group Workshop of the Film Form staged a historic performance to advance their program. One of the rooms we shot in normally has works by the pioneering Constructivist artist Katarzyna Kobro on display. In the 1920s Kobro proposed a radical sculpture with no fixed orientation, no front or back, top or bottom—the works are shown on special glass pedestals—and that inspired us to experiment with making shapes with our bodies during filming. Then I asked the camerawoman, "How would you film if you didn't have a particular viewpoint?" So we talked it over and she chose to shoot the scene with a really loose camera, bending down and shooting up through the glass pedestals.

AM: And now one of the locations in your new work [*of girls*, 2022] is the former home of the writer Fumiko Hayashi. There's a huge cinematic history of the Japanese home. What does it mean for you to shoot in one?

WvO: You know something funny? The cinematographer Yukiko Iioka asked me whether I wanted to shoot with a low viewpoint, and I had to think, well, can I afford to? Because that's what Ozu is known for. The whole world knows it. But I think we have to use a low viewpoint,

because the film crew will be stationed outside and we can only look up from there. Japanese houses are so modular and open that it feels like you always have the possibility of looking through them and out again in many directions. So the camera will be positioned outside the house looking in and through while the figures move about inside.

I think it's fascinating that Fumiko designed her own home. It's like she's a writer who has written her own house, and I want to read the house and analyze the decisions Fumiko made through my work.

AM: How do you plan on approaching the other locations?

WvO: The focus at the main location, Moto Eigakan, is on Yuriko Miyamoto and her female companion Yoshiko Yuasa. There it's not so much the architecture that is guiding me as its function as a tiny cinema that dates back to the 1950s, which also nods to Mikio Naruse's film adaptations of Fumiko's stories. Moto Eigakan was recently restored by a group of young architects and has a clubby, bar-type atmosphere with retro furniture. It feels like this is where you would go to have a good time in contemporary Tokyo, and in terms of cinematography it has many interesting formal aspects.

We are also filming a short scene in the Kanagawa Prefectural Library in Yokohama, which was one of Kunio Maekawa's first public projects in the early 1950s. I was looking for a place dedicated to books, reading, and archiving for us to hold a conversation on Fumiko's writings from Japan's occupied territories during the wars in China and the Asia Pacific. Maekawa's postwar modernism somehow reflects the complex web of power relations that this part of Fumiko's work brings to the fore.

AM: What drew you to the two protagonists of the work, Fumiko Hayashi and Yuriko Miyamoto?

WvO: You already mentioned architecture, music, and film, but now I'm dealing with literature, which is a form of expression that was especially used by women and feminist voices in the early 20th century. It was the main channel through which they could express themselves. I wanted to set up a dialogue between Fumiko and Yuriko because they are such contrasting figures and yet happened to live through the same exact epoch. Fumiko came from extreme poverty and worked her way up to being an incredibly successful writer, while Yuriko came from a privileged background and was well educated before declaring her solidarity with those in poverty. Both of them are sympathetic to class problems, but there's a huge difference in how they express their sympathies.

I was really drawn to Fumiko's writing because it's so passionate and raw. She relates to her own femininity or sexuality in an unusually frank yet beautiful way. There's a punk aspect to it that I like. On the other hand, Yuriko is very clear about her politics. She makes stories around politics, which is what Jean-Luc Goddard did too, but it also becomes dogmatic. The odd thing for me is that Yuriko, who lived with another woman for seven years, seemed driven by loyalty to her ideology to deny her queer history. I find that to be complex and strange, since I've always associated socialism with an openness to homosexuality.

Fumiko and Yuriko will not be worked out as full characters, but I feel their attitudes have something to say about politics today and how young people are responding to our times. I looked for excerpts from their texts for the cast to recite, which recalls my early works where I have people reading aloud. Some of the participants have studied the work and lives of the two women, while others are young people who struggle with similar issues of gender, class, and politics. I am excited to see those historical voices resonate through these young people now.

AM: From Trumpism in the United States to Putin's invasion of Ukraine and growing ecological crises around the world, it feels like we're closer than ever to another global-scale conflict, which seemed unthinkable a few decades ago, when the current generation of young adults was just being born.

WvO: Yes, and now it looks as though Italy will vote an unapologetic admirer of Mussolini's fascism into power. Yuriko wrote an essay entitled "Fascism is alive" in 1949. She was well aware that the dangers of right-wing and fascist ideologies were by no means eradicated after the war, and she asks us not to let ourselves be lulled to sleep by a false sense of security. I feel this is something we need to revisit now, and I plan to ask some of the cast members to talk about fascism today. Fumiko's texts offer another resonance, which is more to do with our relation to gender and sexuality today. She can write with a very open attitude toward desire.

AM: How do you work with the cast in each film? It sounds like you took a highly collaborative approach with *obsada*, but do you ever prepare a lot of instructions in advance?

WvO: It varies from project to project, but one constant is that I always have many conversations with the cast in the run up to the shoot. I want them to know what they're part of and why, because their subjectivity and knowledge is important to the realization of the work.

In the shoot itself I'm usually quite prepared with the kind of scene I want to do, so in the case of *obsada*, for example, I asked pairs of cast members to walk around and talk about their choice to enter the film school, and then they just did that, without my knowing what they were going to say, of course. It was quite a surprise to me how openly they spoke and how honestly interested

they were in each other. But there's also room for other kinds of improvisation. Aside from the interactions with the glass pedestals of the Kobro sculptures, the use of colored Plexiglas panels also emerged out of collaborative discussion. I asked the cast to play with the idea of creating a situation where we could all take charge of the image in some way, rather than having it concentrated in a single person's hands. The colored panels became a device for us to make different images together.

Actually, there's a nice anecdote with the new work. One of the cast members of *Two Stones*, Maya, is a Ukrainian translator living in Kharkiv in KhTZ, the location where we were filming, which was co-designed by Lotte Stam-Beese. Maya told me recently that she has a friend who works as an architect in Tokyo, and she suggested that I look her up. It turns out the friend, Veronika, grew up in KhTZ and now works for Kengo Kuma, one of Japan's most important architects. This was such a beautiful combination of facts! I was amazed to find someone from KhTZ here. On top of that, Veronika trained in traditional Japanese architecture for her master's degree, so she is the one who will be "reading" Fumiko's house. She will be moving through the house and analyzing its elements while we film from outside.

AM: How do you see the other cast members contributing to the new work or shaping our understanding of the protagonists?

WvO: Well, each member of the cast has a specific entry into the issues we are raising together. For example, Ariko Kurosawa researched the correspondences between Yuriko Miyamoto and Yoshiko Yuasa and studied their diary entries. She published her findings in a book in 2008 in which she also discusses Yuriko and Yoshiko's romance in relation to the political context of the time. There will also be a conversation between Kiyomi Sokolova-Yamashita

and Greg Dvorak. Sokolova-Yamashita is a literary scholar who researched Fumiko Hayashi's writing during her wartime travels in the colonies, especially Indonesia, while Dvorak is a Tokyo-based researcher of the Pacific region and its histories of coloniality, gender, and domination by different powers. We'll be reading from Fumiko Hayashi's early work and from a story that relates to Indonesia. From Yuriko we will read political texts as well as letters and diary entries relating to her lesbian relationship. All the readings and discussions circle around some five different but related focal points and will take place in three locations with different configurations of the 11 cast members. I'm still not sure how this will end up in the final work, but I know there are many connecting elements and I will just have to find the key for the edit structure as I go.

> AM: I'd like to return to architecture's role in your practice. In addition to featuring architectural spaces in your films, you also often produce architectural interventions into the exhibition space. Sometimes these may take the form of unusual, bleacher-type seating or cinema-like enclosures. For example, when you first presented *Two Stones* at HKW in Berlin, you made an extreme slope for people to sit on, which I imagine must have had a destabilizing effect on viewers.

WvO: At HKW the screen was suspended in the main exhibition hall but the main viewing point was in the balcony area, so viewers had to be elevated above the floor to see the screen over the balcony edge. I thought it would be nice if the slope just kept going up and up. It wasn't intended to have a destabilizing effect, though sometimes things work out that way. In fact, there were multiple modes of engaging with the work at HKW. People sitting on the balcony had the sound and could see the image with

the subtitles, so they had a relationship with the text element of the work, but the image was also visible on its own from other positions. This resulted in an interesting double-jointed structure that I've tried to replicate in other places where I've since shown the work.

> AM: What's your plan for the Museum of Contemporary Art Tokyo?

WvO: The architectural intervention here is going to be quite sensational, almost like the set in *obsada*. We're basically dropping a continuous polygonal partition into the exhibition space to create a lot of other smaller spaces. The partition has windows and sliding doors, which viewers can open themselves, so as you move through the exhibition you start to see things through different frames. That is, the works themselves become characters that are framed by different kinds of apertures. There will be a raised platform for people to sit on in one area, so you can go up or down in the space, while around one of the corners of the original space the passage through becomes quite narrow—a weird space that isn't normally there—and these interventions change your typical bodily engagement with the museum. There will also be a social space with books and other materials. It will be a sort of study room where people can hold activities, like queer reading groups or feminist reading groups.

I really see the architecture as a work in itself this time. It creates different types of spatial and temporal experiences for viewers as they move through the exhibition, so that they're not simply going from one black box to another.

> AM: So your interventions are also driven out of a concern for the subjectivity of the viewer in your exhibitions, not just presenting videos?

WvO: I've always thought of the viewer as an active participant in the work. I want to enable different relationships to form between work and viewer as well as among viewers themselves, because viewers are also on view to each other. They have their own on-stageness—not in a voyeuristic way, it's just that everyone takes their place in a composition. So I want the viewer to have their own space and thought process. It's like a Brechtian play where you are invited to make your own thing out of it, but I want that to happen on a bodily level and not just an intellectual level, which is why the architecture is so important to me.

AM: What has it been like for you researching and developing a project here in Japan, which momentarily, at least, adds a new topos to those I mentioned at the beginning? Has it given you any insight into your interests and approach to artmaking?

WvO: My relation to Japan essentially started in 2016, when I was invited to participate in that year's Aichi Triennale. I was startled when I suddenly remembered that I could count to 10 in Japanese. It was like a children's rhyme to me—my mother taught me to count in Japanese as a child—and it suddenly came back. As a young girl my mother was held in a Japanese internment camp on Java along with many of the other white Dutch nationals who had been living in colonial Indonesia in the 1930s and '40s. She was eight in 1942 when the Japanese invaded and 12 when she came out of confinement, after which her life and education continued in the Netherlands. She was probably made to do exercises in the morning and learned the numbers that way. So one colonial life was being interrupted by another colonizer. Somehow I had never combined this knowledge of my mother's past with my excitement at being invited to Japan, but there it was.
    What I have realized while staying and working

in Japan now is that one's gaze on the triangle of entangle-ments between the Netherlands, Indonesia, and Japan so often seems to be directed and obscured by national politics or national pain or national pride. I am quite aware of what that means with the gaze from the Netherlands toward Asia, but now I am more aware of how different it all looks from the viewpoint of Japan. Yet other pains, prides, and shames organize the gaze and obscure other things here.

Even in our efforts toward decolonizing our perceptions, we are no doubt guided by "the national" in the issues we are trying to unlearn and unravel. I have come to see more and more how this is also an obstruction. So the question remains: What could be a way of working in art that acknowledges the enormous paradigm shifts we are experiencing already—along with the violence that accompanies them? And then how can our work somehow help to guide these shifts in values toward a more balanced way of living together in-and-with this world? I often recall the title of Benjamin Moser's biography of the Brazilian writer Clarice Lispector: *Why This World?* That question says it all.

A condensed version of this interview previously appeared in the exhibition booklet.

Andrew Maerkle

is a writer, editor, and translator based in Tokyo. He is deputy
editor of the online platform ART iT | International Edition
and a contributor to international publications including *frieze*
and *Artforum*. From 2006 to 2008 he was deputy editor of
ArtAsiaPacific magazine in New York. His book of translations
Kishio Suga. Writings, vol. 1, 1969-1979 was published by
Skira in 2021. He teaches in the Graduate School of Global
Arts at Tokyo University of the Arts.

Wendelien van Oldenborgh:

《オブサダ》映像スチル

Film still from *obsada*

Film still from *obsada*

《オブサダ》映像スチル

《偽りなき響き》映像スチル

Film still from No False Echoes

Production still from obsada, photo by Jakub Danilewicz

〈オブサダ〉撮影記録　撮影：ヤコブ・ダニレヴィッチ

Production still from *Hier*, photo by Jakub Danilewicz

《ヒア》撮影記録　撮影：ヤコブ・ダニレヴィッチ

《彼女たちの》映像スチル（ラッシュフィルムより）

Still from the film rushes of of girls

《彼女たちの》映像スチル

Film still from of girls

Film still from *Two Stones*

List of works

Maurits Script —————————————— 116

No False Echoes —————————————— 118

Two Stones ——————————————— 120

Hier. ————————————————— 122

obsada ———————————————— 124

of girls ———————————————— 126

Footnotes to: obsada (2022)
Lenticular print (a set of two), 120 x 180 cm

Footnotes to: of girls (2022)
Lenticular print (a set of two), 120 x 300 cm

Two-channel film installation in
architectural setting, and booklet,
26 minutes and 38 minutes

Maurits Script (2006)

read and discussed by:
Anthony Clarke artist, tailor, pattern
cutter for jeans wear
Romeo K. Gambier DJ, radio host
Charl Landvreugd artist, theorist of
contemporary art, lecturer
Eunice Landvreugd nurse,
home carer
Cristiane de Morais Smith
theoretical physicist
Peter Olsthoorn political scientist,
writer, lecturer
Nienke Terpsma artist, graphic designer
Alexander Vollebregt urbanist, lecturer

camera: **Joris Kerbosch**,
Sal Kroonenberg
sound: **Martijn van Haalen**
filmed on location:
Museum Het Mauritshuis,
The Hague, the Netherlands

produced by: **Casco Utrecht**

Maurits Script takes as its starting point the Dutch colonial past in northeast Brazil, a history that is frequently overlooked in the Netherlands. Van Oldenborgh constructed a script around the figure of Johan Maurits of Nassau, the Dutch governor in Brazil from 1637 to 1644, who is highly regarded by the Dutch as an early humanist ruler. Compiled from original sources, ranging from personal letters to political council minutes, the script paints a complex portrait of the conflicts of the time, including tensions between Portuguese and Dutch colonizers, and the less-recognized aspects of Maurits's governance, such as his treatment of slaves and the indigenous population.

As the title suggests, the film is about script work, more precisely about voicing and embodying many voices and experiences, not without political or ideological difficulty. Van Oldenborgh invited participants with different personal relationships to the issues raised. The reading of the historical words opens up a space for criticism toward inherited voices and gives other voices a place to speak up.

Maurits Script was filmed as a one-day public event in the Golden Room of the Mauritshuis museum, Maurits's former residence in The Hague. On one side of the room, the participants individually read their lines, while on the other the remaining participants engaged in conversation around a table. The latter group addressed the legacies of colonial histories within contemporary Dutch society, in particular concerning citizenship and multiculturalism, at times revealing conflicting viewpoints. Over the course of the day, the conversation took on momentum, growing to involve the camera crew and the audience.

Film installation with two acoustic panels, 30 minutes

No False Echoes (2008)

voices and appearances by:
Salah Edin is a rapper whose lyrics, in Dutch and Arabic, often deal with perceptions of immigrants in Dutch society. The Dutch politician Geert Wilders, in his 2008 film *Fitna*, mistakenly used a photo of Edin to depict Mohammed Bouyeri, the murderer of filmmaker Theo van Gogh.
Edwin Jurriëns is a lecturer at the University of New South Wales and the author of *From Monologue to Dialogue: Radio and Reform in Indonesia* (2010), among other books. His research focuses on radio and other forms of Indonesian popular media in the context of globalization.
Wim Noordhoek is a Dutch radio programmer, journalist, and author. Since 1967 he has regularly made programs that give alternative music serious airtime. In 2000 Noordhoek made a series of programs for the VPRO (Liberal Protestant Radio Broadcaster) radio about the PHOHI (Philips Holland-Indies Broadcasting Station), using original recordings that had been preserved on 78s by the Philips Concern Archives.

Baukje Prins is an associate professor of citizenship and diversity at the Hague University of Applied Sciences and author of *Beyond Innocence: The Debate on Integration in the Netherlands* (2004) and *Accidental Classmates: Life Stories at the Intersection of Ethnicity, Class, Gender and Religion* (2014).
Joss Wibisono is chief editor of the Indonesian Section of Radio Netherlands, where he has worked since 1987, and an expert on Dutch-Indonesian relations with an emphasis on the influence of gamelan (Balinese and Javanese traditional music) on Western music. He wrote his PhD dissertation on the Indonesian nationalist Soewardi Soerjaningrat.
Lina Campanella was an eight-year-old singer at the time of filming, having just started her training in the national youth choir Vocaal Talent Nederland.

camera: **Joris Kerbosch**, **Michael Brooke**
sound: **Ludo Engels**, **Peter Cue**
filmed on location: **Radio Kootwijk**, Apeldoorn, the Netherlands

produced by: **Van Abbemuseum**

List of works

In Europe, radio developed as a state-controlled instrument for edifying the masses through speeches and lectures. *No False Echoes* recalls this history of radio and specifically revisits Dutch radio in colonial-era Indonesia. The Philips company not only exported radio technology to the colony in the late 1920s, but also produced the programs to ensure that the content would be innocent and uplifting, and to keep un-wanted political voices off the ether. While the Dutch colonizers were finding nostalgic comfort in reports about the traditional December celebrations of St. Nicolas, the Indonesian people were busy develop-ing their own nationalist self-awareness. *No False Echoes* deals with these simultaneous yet opposing movements, against the background of the current revival of nationalist sentiments in the Netherlands.

The setting is the former main building of Radio Kootwijk, an architectural monument to modernism and progress, and the first broadcast station to send radio messages to the former Dutch Indies. Yet, it is also clearly a building that has lost its function and has been empty for several years. The voices in *No False Echoes* are not improvising or searching, but rather assertive, at times almost didac-tic, fitting the nature of a radio program. As in a radio talk show, the Dutch perspective is discussed by two experts on history and an analyst of today's political tendencies. The voice of the Indonesian independence movement is represented by a political pamphlet from 1913, "If I Were a Dutchman." This provocative manifesto is recited by Salah Edin, a Moroccan Dutch rap artist known for his biting criticism of contemporary perceptions of immigrants. The work was filmed with an invited audience and speakers who cite from history as well as converse spontaneously about the issues at hand.

Single-channel film installation with
two soundtracks and subtitles,
28 minutes each

Two Stones (2019)

dialogues and appearances by:
Hannah Dawn Henderson artist,
writer, the Hague, the Netherlands
Ievgeniia Gubkina architect, activist,
writer, Kharkiv, Ukraine
Maya Smolnyaninova translator,
Kharkiv
Ola Hassanain artist, architect,
Utrecht, the Netherlands
and Khartoum, Sudan
Hanneke Oosterhof biographer of
Lotte Stam-Beese, Woensdrecht,
the Netherlands

and:
Roman Budetskiy
Sofiya Dybok
Andriy Khlebnikov
Dmytro Bulakh
Natalya Doroshchuk
Jolanda Renfurm

camera: **Maasja Ooms**
sound recording: **Rik Meier**
sound mix: **Titus Maderlechner**
filmed on location: **KhTZ**, Kharkiv,
Pendrecht, Rotterdam

produced by: **Fabian Altenried** for
Schuldenberg Films
supported by: **bauhaus imaginista**

Two Stones explores the trajectories and ideals of the Bauhaus-trained German architect Lotte Stam-Beese and the Caribbean activist and writer Hermina Huiswoud through dialogues and appearances by contemporary protagonists. Both Stam-Beese and Huiswoud spent time working in the Soviet Union in the early 1930s, and both were active in the Netherlands after World War II. *Two Stones* was filmed in the Constructivist district of KhTZ in Kharkiv, Ukraine, the first large housing project on which Stam-Beese worked in the 1930s, and in Stam-Beese's celebrated 1950s residential area known as Pendrecht, designed during her period as Rotterdam's main architect and urban planner. In the 1970s, Huiswoud was agitating against a Rotterdam housing law that prohibited Caribbean Dutch inhabitants from settling in any of the city's districts if their presence would exceed five percent of the population. Resonances as well as dissonances between the two women's trajectories and their relationships to socialist ideology are sensed through the thoughts and experiences of the protagonists, who all have a personal or professional relation to the issues at hand.

Filmed in 2018, the film work superimposes the images of the two locations. Spatially and rhythmically the locations display similarities. The installation's formal characteristic of fitting two different sound tracks to one image edit, adds to this superimposition. On a social level, notions of stigmatization and segregation that apply to both neighborhoods also produce echoes and reverberations between them.

Four-channel video wall with
wooden frame, 27 minutes

Hier. (2021)

text, dialogue, music,
and appearances by:
Pelumi Adejumo writes fiction,
poetry and theater. The text she
reads was written especially for *Hier*.
Lara Nuberg researches, writes,
and speaks about the colonial past
of the Netherlands and Indonesia.
FRED features **Lyana Usa**, lead
guitarist, singer-songwriter, and
student of electrical engineering
at Delft Technical University;
Josephine Spit, bassist and student
of architecture at Delft Technical
University; and **Thirza Hiwat**,
drummer, multi-instrumentalist,
and student of information science
at Utrecht University.

camera: **Lawrence Lee Kalkman**
sound recording: **Roel Pothoven**
sound mix: **Tyler Friedman**
filmed on location: **Museum Arnhem**,
under renovation, Arnhem,
the Netherlands

produced with: **Hannah Dawn
Henderson**
supported by: **Sonsbeek20->24**

Hier. moves seamlessly between politically charged reflections and personal memories through a constellation of voices and lyrical material. In the under-renovation Museum Arnhem in the Netherlands —a place of conservation in transition—a cast of young women express themselves through music, poetry, and dialogue. Together they sensitively explore themes such as hybridity, transnationality, and diasporic sensitivities: the political instrumentalization of identity and cultural renewal in the midst of persistent reverberations of colonial history in contemporary society.

The location is also a meaningful "voice." Museum Arnhem was founded in the late 19th century as an "outdoors club," a gentlemen's club, by residents of Arnhem who did not have sufficient social status to join the more prestigious Groote Sociëteit. Many were people with a colonial past. The film shows the building stripped down to its foundation, with worn concrete and elegant Art Nouveau features juxtaposed. In this contrasting site of rubble and potential, three "sonic lines" manifest: the band FRED develops an improvisation of traditional Indonesian kroncong music before moving into their own contemporary song; Pelumi Adejumo reads a text she wrote as a result of her conversations with the other members of the cast; and Lara Nuberg spontaneously reacts to various documents, statements, the music, and the building itself. Through music and poetry, we encounter not only sociopolitical urgencies, but also undercurrents of existentialism and vulnerability. Tender yet confident, the protagonists display friendship and cooperation, and tell of love and its sorrows, questions, and certainties, by which they express the basis for a changing possible future.

obsada (2021)

dialogue and appearances by:
Magdalena Bojdo cinematographer,
Warsaw, Poland
Paulina Sacha sound director,
midwife, Warsaw and Berlin, Germany
Monika Czajkowska director,
producer, lecturer, Warsaw
Ewa Borysiewicz director,
screenwriter, visual artist, Warsaw
Magda Kupryjanowicz playwright,
screenwriter, Warsaw
Elżbieta Szurpicka costume designer,
set designer, Warsaw
Aleksandra Rosset editor, Łódź, Poland
Joanna Sokolowska curator, Łódź

camera: **Magdalena Bojdo**
sound: **Paulina Sacha**
filmed on location:
Muzeum Sztuki w Łodzi,
Łódź Film School, Łódź, Poland

produced with:
Jakub Danilewicz, **Monika Czajkowska**
produced and supported by:
Muzeum Sztuki w Łodzi, **Virtual
Narratives Lab of the Łódź Film
School** and **Mondriaan Fonds**

In Polish, the title of this work, *obsada*, can connote variously a film cast, group work, or putting a plant in the ground. Here it refers to a group of female students and graduates of Poland's National Film School, and professional women film crew members, filming each other and talking about various aspects of their work in the school and the Muzeum Sztuki in Łódź. The two institutions provide specific historical references and contexts to their dialogue; one such is an all-male avant-garde group inspired by Russian Constructivism, Workshop of the Film Form (1970–1977), founded by artists and students from the film school to break away from the classical education and bridge cinema and contemporary art. In 1973, Workshop of the Film Form organized a 23-day event titled Workshop Action in the museum to implement their ideas regarding the expansion of cinematography, production, authorship, and the pedagogy of art.

In the process of filming in collaboration with Van Oldenborgh, the cast and film crew improvised a series of actions inspired by Workshop of the Film Form as well as the female Constructivist sculptor Katarzyna Kobro (1898–1951), whose work embodied the idea of infinite space without any preferred point of view. They discuss how patriarchal privilege, which the earlier avant-garde movement failed to recognize and still persists today, deeply influences the formation of their subjectivity and aspirations in the cultural field. The assemblage of their voices and actions in *obsada* signals change —change that has happened or is yet to come, while simultaneously embodying the idea of collaboration and openness in working modes.

Single channel film installation,
40 minutes

# of girls (2022)

read and discussed by:
aliwen artist, curator, writer, graduate student of Global Arts, Tokyo University of the Arts, Tokyo, Japan
Greg Dvorak artist, writer, researcher of Pacific and Asia, gender and coloniality, author of *Coral and Concrete : Remembering Kwajalein Atoll Between Japan, America, and the Marshall Islands* (2018), Tokyo
Hanna Hirakawa artist, curator, graduate student of Global Arts, Tokyo University of the Arts, Tokyo
Veronika Ikonnikova artist, architect, Tokyo
Ariko Kurosawa researcher of contemporary Japanese/Okinawan and feminist literature and queer theories, and the editor of *Letters between Yuriko Miyamoto and Yoshiko Yuasa* (2008, untranslated), Okinawa, Japan
Chelsea Szendi Schieder researcher of contemporary histories of activism and gender, author of *Coed Revolution: The Female Student in the Japanese New Left* (2021), Tokyo
Kiyomi Sokolova-Yamashita researcher of contemporary Japanese literature, author of *Fumiko Hayashi and Indonesia: Work and Research* (2022, untranslated), Tokyo
Mariko Tamura curator, Museum of Contemporary Art Tokyo, Tokyo
Kanae Tanikawa artist, stray researcher, member of artist-duo MES, FAQ?, and NEON BOOK CLUB, Tokyo
Yiqing DJ, organizer of ether, member of NEON BOOK CLUB, Tokyo
Miyu Yokota actor, member of artist collective the fuu, Tokyo

texts recited from:
· Fumiko Hayashi, *Aouma wo mitari* [I saw a pale horse], Tokyo: Nihon Tosho Center, 2002 (English translation from *I Saw a Pale Horse and Selected Poems from Diary of a Vagabond*, translated by J. Brown, New York: Cornell University East Asia Program, 1997).
· Fumiko Hayashi, *Horoki fukugenban* [Diary of a Vagabond, Restored Version], edited by Kenji Hirohata, Tokyo: Ronsosha, 2012 (English translation from Joan E. Ericson, *Be a Woman: Hayashi Fumiko and Modern Japanese Women's Literature*, Honolulu: University of Hawaii Press, 1997).
· Ariko Kurosawa, *Ofuku-shokan: Miyamoto Yuriko to Yuasa Yoshiko* [Letters between Yuriko Miyamoto and Yoshiko Yuasa], Tokyo: Kanrin Shobo, 2008.
· Yuriko Miyamoto, "Fashizumu wa ikiteiru [Fascism is alive]," *Heiwa wa nemuri wo yurusanai* [Peace permits no sleep], Tokyo: Shin-Nihon Shuppan, 1989.
· Yuriko Miyamoto, "Chibusa [Breasts]," *Miyamoto Yuriko senshuu* [Anthology of Yuriko Miyamoto], Vol. 3, Tokyo: Shin-Nihon Shuppan, 1968.

camera: **Yukiko Iioka**
camera assistant and lighting: **Yoshio Kitagawa**, **Takuya Murakami**
sound recording: **Young Chang Hwang, Ryota Fujiguchi**
sound mix: **Ryota Fujiguchi**
line producer: **Natsuko Odate** (**Yoshiko Issiki Office**)
filmed on location: **Hayashi Fumiko Memorial Hall**, **Kanagawa Prefectural Library**, **Moto Eigakan**

produced and supported by:
Museum of Contemporary Art Tokyo, **Mondriaan Fonds**

Filmed in Tokyo and Yokohama, *of girls* brings
a variety of contemporary voices in resonance with
two distinct female voices from Japan's literary and
political past. Both popular authors of their time
—the period from the late 1920s on—Fumiko Hayashi
(1903–1951) and Yuriko Miyamoto (1899–1951) both
died young in the same year. They each had a strong
feminist and class consciousness as well as an impressive literary voice, but came from very different
backgrounds and expressed their ideals through
different paths.

Born to a deprived family, Fumiko Hayashi
made her name as an author with semi-autobiographical fiction novels and poetries, in which she openly
expressed a sense of female class solidarity and sexual
desire. With her success she eventually designed and
built her own house in Shinjuku, Tokyo. During the
wars, she was sent by the Imperial Army and major
newspapers to the occupied territories—among them
Indonesia—and contributed various articles and poems.

Yuriko Miyamoto is remembered for the
political rigor of her writings and life that pursued
socialist ideals and women's liberation. She was born
into a privileged family, and married a Japanese man,
but left him after meeting the researcher of Russian
literature, writer and openly lesbian Yoshiko Yuasa.
For seven years Miyamoto lived with Yuasa, and
wrote several novels about their relationship. Later
Miyamoto married the socialist leader Kenji
Miyamoto and continued supporting him in prison,
while she herself was imprisoned various times.

The power and contradictions in both these
women's words reverberate in dialogues and images
of an intergenerational cast moving through the
various spaces of knowledge, memory and culture,
and reflect today's struggles around gender, politics,
and love.

Exhibition

wendelien van oldenborgh
unset on-set

12 November 2022–19 February 2023
Museum of Contemporary Art Tokyo, Exhibition Gallery 3F

Organized by Museum of Contemporary Art Tokyo
operated by Tokyo Metropolitan Foundation for History and Culture

Supported by Mondriaan Fonds and
Embassy of the Kingdom of the Netherlands

Curator: Kyongfa Che (Museum of Contemporary Art Tokyo)

Curatorial Assistant: Mariko Tamura (Museum of Contemporary
Art Tokyo), Hanna Hirakawa, Satoshi Aoki (Intern)

Press Officer: Chiako Kudo, Yurano Uchibori,
Tomoko Inaba (Museum of Contemporary Art Tokyo)

Construction and display: HIGURE 17-15 cas

Acknowledgment

We would like to express our sincere gratitude to all the following institutions and individuals for their generous assistance and contributions to the realization of this exhibition. (Honorifics omitted)

Wendelien van Oldenborgh

Mondriaan Fonds,
Embassy of the Kingdom of the Netherlands

Kota Abe, Ryuta Akamatsu, aliwen, Toshihiko Arimoto, Binna Choi, Jakub Danilewicz, Pablo de Ocampo, Greg Dvorak, Manami Eguchi, Ryota Fujiguchi, Mio Harada, Hanna Hirakawa, Young Chang Hwang, Yukiko Iioka, Veronika Ikonnikova, Asako Iwama, Yuka Kanno, Yoshio Kitagawa, Ariko Kurosawa, Andrew Maerkle, Takuya Murakami, Natsuko Odate, Tadamasa Okamura, Akira Rachi, Hiromi Sawabe, Chelsea Szendi Schieder, Tetsuro Shimauchi, Tomoko Shimizu, SHION, Kiyomi Sokolova-Yamashita, Hiroshi Suzuki, Obiko Takehana, Noriko Takeichi, Kanae Tanikawa, Ayaka Ura, Akiko Wakabayashi, Yiqing, Miyu Yokota

CubeFilm Inc., etc.books, the fuu, Hayashi Fumiko Memorial Hall, Kanagawa Prefectural Library, Moto Eigakan, NEON BOOK CLUB, Stranger, Sumida Mukojima Expo, Yoshiko Isshiki Office

Catalogue

wendelien van oldenborgh
unset on-set

First published in Japan, 28th December, 2022

Supervised by Museum of Contemporary Art Tokyo

Texts by Yuka Kanno, Binna Choi, Pablo de Ocampo,
Andrew Maerkle, Kyongfa Che

Art direction by Akiko Wakabayashi

Editing by Satoko Shibahara, Nao Amino (torch press)

Editorial assistant by Mariko Tamura, Hanna Hirakawa,
Satoshi Aoki, Nanako Toriya (torch press)

Translation by Matt Treyvaud (EN pp. 23–33),
Yuka Katagiri (JP pp. 43–58, 81 [Bio]),
Haruko Kohno (JP pp. 67–81), Akira Rachi (JP pp. 91–106),
Hanna Hirakawa / Kyongfa Che (JP pp. 116–126)

English proofreading by Lindsey Westbrook
(except pp. 23–34, 91–106)

Photography (Installation views) by Kenji Morita

Printed and bound in Japan by Hakkou Bijyutsu

ISBN 978-4-907562-38-0

Published by torch press
1959 Enzan Fujiki, Koshu, Yamanashi pref., 404-0054 Japan
torchpress.net | order@torchpress.net

Text © 2022 Kyongfa Che, Yuka Kanno, Binna Choi,
Pablo de Ocampo, Andrew Maerkle
© 2022 Wendelien van Oldenborgh, torch press

Film still from *Two Stones*

〈ふたつの石〉映像スチル

《偽りなき響き》映像スチル

Film still from *No False Echoes*

《ヒア》撮影記録　撮影：ヤコブ・ダニレヴィッチ

Production still from *Hier.*, photo by Jakub Danilewicz

Film still from *Maurits Script*

〈マウリッツ・スクリプト〉映像スチル

《彼女たちの》映像スチル

Film still from of girls